A YEAR IN CHRISTINE'S GARDEN

A Year in Christine's Garden is the utterly down-to-earth account of one woman's passion for plants. Recounting stories from her hectic life in horticulture, Christine Walkden's diary is a heartwarming account of octogenerian neighbours, living with a film crew and helping friends with their gardening needs.

Reflecting all the charm of her BBC2 television series, Christine's narrative paints a picture of the day-to-day beauty that surrounds her. She likes being outside, she likes walking her dog Tara, she likes watching the light change and she enjoys those little moments when everything seems right in the world.

As the year progresses, this warm but frank diary brings to life all the moments of pride, excitement, relaxation and laugh-out-loud fun that make Christine's garden a haven of contentment.

A YEAR IN CHRISTINE'S GARDEN

The Secret Diary of a Garden Lover

Christine Walkden

LARGE
PRINT

First published 2007
by
Ebury Publishing
This Large Print edition published 2007
by
BBC Audiobooks Ltd
by arrangement with
Ebury Publishing, an imprint of the Random
House Group

UK Hardcover ISBN 978 1 405 64865 3
UK Softcover   ISBN 978 1 405 64866 0

British Library Cataloguing in Publication Data available

Printed and bound in Great Britain by
Antony Rowe Ltd., Chippenham, Wiltshire

To Rupert, Jimmy, Laurie, Kate and Sarah

CONTENTS

ACKNOWLEDGEMENTS

A special mention must go to Rupert, Jimmy, Laurie, Kate and Sarah. You all know what it took to film and edit *Christine's Garden*. I know what you all gave. I pass on to you all my love, gratitude, thanks and appreciation.

My sincere thanks and appreciation must also be expressed to everyone who has made the filming and production of *Christine's Garden* so successful. You all know who you are and what you all did for me.

Everyone at the BBC: those that worked with me during the filming, those people that let me film with them, and the people who looked after Tara—all added a significant amount to the production of the series. I must drive Penny McLeish mad at times but I value everything you do for me.

I would have to include so many names that I would be in danger of missing someone, so I hope you will all accept my thanks knowing that I am grateful and thrilled that you all contributed in a series that we can all be proud of.

To all the people at BBC Books who have worked on this book and those who worked with me personally, I express my thanks and gratitude— your work, enthusiasm and efforts are acknowledged and fully valued.

Love and thanks to you all and continue to enjoy your gardens and plants.

INTRODUCTION

My first memory of being interested in plants goes back to when I was at school in Blackburn, Lancashire. Each autumn every child was given a yoghurt pot, some compost and a crocus corm to plant. These were put carefully under the stairs— and then mine always got looked after by someone other than me. That used to annoy me like nothing else.

Then one day near the end of the summer term the headmistress came into the classroom and asked if any child would take a houseplant home with them for the holidays as the school would be closed for the summer. I immediately stuck my hand up and took three home. My dad went nuts and said we were not taking these plants with us on our annual holiday!

I do not remember why or how I knew to do what I then did, but I took the plants to our shed and put them on bricks standing in water in a tin bath. I then shut the shed door, plunging the plants into almost total darkness and went away for two weeks' holiday.

When I came home I rushed to the shed, thinking that the plants would be dead, but to my delight when I opened the door they were in full bloom and looked fantastic. I was only ten years old, but I had to find out why this happened. I'm still not sure! In fact, to this day I have never managed to repeat it, but I do know that it was this experience that started me off.

Next I grew cress, carrot tops and seeds on my

bedroom windowsill, then moved outside into the back yard and grew plants in pots. There was no soil in the yard, which was paved.

One day I went down the allotments near home and found a neglected site and asked a lady standing by it whose it was. She said it was her late husband's, and I remember asking her what she meant by late. Once I got over that, I asked if I could have it. She told me that it was rented from the council offices. Off I went, and before too long was the proud owner of a weed- and bramble-congested plot.

I was only ten, so my parents had to rent it, but it was mine—my first bit of land—and on it I grew flowers and vegetables which I then sold to the locals. Later, when I was at secondary school, I used to take produce into school and sell it to the teachers. It was on this plot that I realized that I could do this as a job when I grew up.

On leaving school I spent a year at the Clitheroe parks department, getting in some practical experience before going to the Lancashire College of Agriculture to complete a three-year diploma. My sandwich year was spent working with shrubs, weed-killers, beetroot and rhubarb!

But it was by no means the end of my study, which continued both at school and on the job. I finished the diploma and moved to Kew to work on the practical side of the seed physiology unit at Wakehurst Place in West Sussex. I then moved to Llangollen, in North Wales, to work for Dobies, Carter, Cuthbert and Dom, the seedsmen, as a technical adviser. From there I went to the Rhondda valley to set up a training workshop for the Manpower Services Commission.

I then decided I wanted to extend my professional qualifications, so I went to both Pershore and Writtle colleges before becoming a lecturer in horticulture at Capel Manor in Enfield, north London. From there I went to the Baby Bio Company as an advisory manager for the garden products division.

The major change to my career happened a couple of years after that, when I decided that I wanted to go freelance. I was already lecturing nationally and internationally; I was carrying out consultancies for gardeners and professional horticulturalists; I had started to do a bit of television for the BBC and ITV, and was taking part in live phone-ins on several local radio stations; and I was also leading garden tours and botanical trips all around the world. I felt that trying to keep what was amounting to two jobs down was killing me, so I left regular employment and went self-employed.

And I haven't looked back. I love what I do and the varying nature of my work. I do not have a regular work pattern, as each week is different. It is that constant changing environment that stimulates me.

I now work any day of the week that people wish me to, and I frequently work weekends as well. I lecture around the country, train professionals in both craft and management skills, work in nurseries, garden centres and farmers' markets as a consultant in marketing, merchandising and display, and give advice and training to super-market staff on organics, flowers and house plant care. I am a correspondence tutor to various organizations, an assessor for various trade bodies, and a business adviser for a local council. I carry out plant designs for people, and I still garden for a number of clients I have looked after for many years.

I also lead garden tours and my own trips into the wilds to see and photograph wild flowers around the world, and broadcast on a number of national and local radio stations.

Being self-employed has meant that I have been able to make time to focus on my own home—in Hertfordshire, where I live with my dog Tara. The garden is long and thin, measuring 53 x 10.5m (175 x 35 feet), and in it I grow flowers, trees, shrubs, alpines, bulbs, climbers and vegetables. I have a patio where in the summer there are over 90 containers, and the house is home to more than 250 house plants. I eat, dream and breathe gardening, and would not want to do anything else. I am incredibly lucky.

✳

Have you ever wondered what it must be like to pick up a phone and be told that it is the BBC calling? Well, that's what happened, in late December 2004, when a past contact at the BBC phoned to ask if I would be willing to do some filming with her for a possible new TV programme.

At that stage she would not tell me anything else, other than to say that she would like to bring a small film crew to film with me in the New Year. She was looking for enthusiasm and passion. That's all she said. Eventually, having tried all sorts of things to find out what she was up to, I arranged to do some filming with her on 11 January 2005. All she asked for was for me to interview someone I knew, do a bit of filming in my garden and then just chat to the camera.

I was not totally happy about this. I had no idea what it was for, or what the BBC was thinking of, and she was not telling me. Unfortunately, in the past, I had experienced circumstances that left me very unsure about this lady, and I was not convinced by what she was saying about wanting to capture my passion and enthusiasm.

The other, even greater, problem for me was I was very, very unsure if I actually wanted to be involved with television at all. I am a private person and was very concerned about the consequences of making a television programme. I must say that I was not convinced about it all.

Twenty years ago, if someone had offered me the opportunity to do some filming for a possible programme I would have probably taken her hand off in my enthusiasm. Now, age and contentment with my present lifestyle, plus having had my fingers burned in the past by programme-makers, has changed things considerably.

Television sounds great. What a life! But you soon come to realize that, as with everything in life, there is reality and perception, and so often the perception is very far removed from the reality of the situation. Television is just that, for me.

In practice it means hard work, and long and often unsociable hours. You are left very tired, to the extent that after a day's filming you do not want to do anything other than go to bed. Days can be long and demanding. You have to have the patience of a saint, and be very tolerant of requests to repeat things time and time again.

I am not saying that you do not have fun as well,

because, if you have the right crew around you, you do. But I found my first series very difficult, as I did not have a clue what was expected of me or what I should be doing.

On 11 January the film crew turned up, and, as had been requested by the lady who was acting as the director, I interviewed someone I knew. Enter Reg Walker! Reg is one of my neighbours, and I have a very special relationship with him and his wife, Pat. I have known them since I moved into my house some 15 years ago. Reg and I share our plants and produce, and Reg walks my dog, Tara, for me on a daily basis. Even though he is deaf, I felt very comfortable about interviewing him in front of a camera.

We went round to Reg's, and the director just asked me to chat to him about anything I wanted to, and that's what I did. I cannot even remember what we chatted about. Anyway, after a while, she said she was happy and could we now go and film in my garden.

We went up into the vegetable garden, where not a lot was growing, apart from leeks, swedes, brussels sprouts and green manure. The director asked me to chat to the camera about brussels sprouts! This I managed with considerable ease, and I didn't mention farting once in the whole piece. I suppose that's because they do not have that effect on me—unlike some people—and I am a great fan of the crop. I even eat them raw in salads during the winter.

The director then asked me to stand in my kitchen and chat to her about gardening, what I liked about it, and my life. At one stage she asked me about the spirituality of gardening, and I replied that I did not think at that level. She then told me that everything I had said was on that level. This surprised me enormously, and I said, 'In which case it comes straight from the heart and not from the head.' Having completed that filming, she then asked me to go into my living-room, and to look out of the window and talk about what I saw.

I chatted away about the trees that grow in front of my house and what I felt about them. After a short time, she said she had seen enough and did not need anything else. I asked her what it was for, but she just kept saying she was looking for 'enthusiasm and passion'. How those three words were to haunt me over the next few months. She left saying she would be in contact fairly soon.

It was 7 February before I heard again from the director. She said people from the BBC, in Birmingham, were very happy about what they had seen and liked Reg very much. Once again she said she would be in touch, and once again I asked her what it was for. All I got back was those, now irritating, three words. It did not tell me what they were up to at all. The year before this diary begins was to be a huge learning curve for me.

9 February. The director was on the phone again saying that the taster tape was now in London and, if they liked what they saw, it would be six half-hour programmes. I thought: great, but about what? At this stage I was getting very frustrated by all this mystery, and lack of consideration in not telling me what was going on. I could not get anything out of the director at all. This was beginning to annoy me a lot.

23 February. The director phoned me sounding very excited indeed. She said the BBC had commissioned me to do a six-part series for BBC2. She was much more excited than I was, because I still did not have a clue as to what had been commissioned. I told the director that I was not happy about not knowing what they had commissioned, and what I was being asked to do. She said she would come and see me and explain things then.

This news left me feeling extremely unsettled. I had no idea what I was being offered, apart from that fact that it was six half-hour programmes on BBC2 on a Friday night. Well, there was a clue, I suppose—Friday night must be gardening, but that's all I knew.

28 February. Yet another phone call. The director would be coming to see me shortly, with the BBC Executive Producer of Gardening for BBC2. No date was set, and I was just left waiting and wondering what was going on. The next thing that happened was that Nick Patten, the executive producer, was on the phone having a chat to me. He said he and the director would like to come and see me. I tried asking him what it all was about, but still the only thing I got back was those three words!

By this stage I was losing interest and was getting irritated by these silly phone calls that actually said nothing. I do not work in the land of mystery. My feet are too much on the ground, and I was getting to the stage where I wanted to know exactly what was going on, and what they wanted me to do. By now I had experienced two months of all this stuff but still did not have a clue.

16 March. A lady from BBC contracts spoke to me about the series, but in such terms that she too still gave nothing away. All she said was that the BBC would like to offer me a contract to make a series that would be shown on BBC2. Once again I was told that the director and executive producer would be coming to see me. The director phoned me and asked if she and Nick Patten could come to see me on 18 March. I thought that the only way that I was going to find out was to let them come.

18 March. The two of them appeared and still talked in very general terms. Nick was keen to try and establish the sort of film crew I could work with. I told him that I wanted a team who were interested in people rather than TV. My past experiences had left me very aware that some TV crews are only interested in making their programmes and have little time for the people involved. Once the two left, and I had time to think about what had been said, I still was not clear about what they wanted.

22 March. The BBC contracts department spoke to me again. I did not get any more detail! They were now talking money, but I did not know what they wanted from me, so we did not progress very well.

30 March. I phoned Nick and told him my garden was starting to look nice, so did he want to start filming? He did not seem very keen, which left me feeling a bit frustrated and in the dark.

11 April. A BBC contract appeared on my doorstep and, for the first time, I got an inkling of what they wanted. This worried me, as it said it was a contract for an 'observational documentary' to be filmed over 60 days. I thought I was being asked to do a gardening programme. I spoke to Nick about this, and he told me not to worry as he was trying to find a producer/director who would explain everything to me. Nick also said that he would come to see me again on 27 May.

9 May. Nick phoned me to say that he had found someone he thought I would get on well with. His name was Rupert Miles.

23 May. Rupert Miles phoned for a chat while I was out. He sounded excited and left a message on my answerphone to ring him back. Unfortunately, he did not leave his number. I thought, 'here's a right one!'

Over the next few days, Rupert and I exchanged e-mails and phone calls, and I formed the impression that he was a sensitive, caring person who had a wide range of interests, many of which were similar to my own.

27 May. Nick and Rupert came to see me. Nick left after lunch, and then Rupert and I talked about all sorts of things, mainly trying to get to know each other and explore what we might, possibly, achieve. Once Nick had left, I asked Rupert directly what the BBC wanted of me and, once again, out came the same three words. I got annoyed and asked him, please, to try and find out. What did they want me to do?

We then went round to Reg and Louise's, so I could introduce Rupert to my neighbours. We sat on the patio, got the wine out and talked about programme-making, and Rupert's background. At the end of the evening I felt happy with Rupert but still was not a lot closer to knowing what they wanted. Frustrating!

Between the end of May and 21 June I had various conversations with Rupert, and met the assistant producer, Kate Hollingsworth. She seemed a nice person, and I felt I would be able to work with her. I also decided in my own mind that the BBC did not know what it wanted and it was down to Rupert and me to make the series. This concerned me a lot, but Rupert kept telling me it would be OK.

21 June. My first day filming with Rupert and Kate in my home. I was apprehensive, and had such mixed feelings. Could I do what they wanted? Would it be OK? What were we going to film? Should I be doing it? Would I like it? In my mind I was all over the place. There was a certain amount of panic going on. In practice, Rupert and Kate spent the first day filming the garden, not me.

At one stage in the day, I felt frustrated having them in my home and garden. I have lived the vast majority of my life on my own, and to have two people around all day, filming, was a new experience. I felt comfortable with them as people, but was not sure about the rest.

In the evening I was uncertain about the filming planned for the next morning. Rupert had asked me not to get dressed but to stay in my pyjamas and dressing-gown. This is what I normally do first thing, while looking around my garden, but I was not at all happy with the thought that the viewers were going to see me!

22 June. I decided that I would try to see if I felt OK with being filmed, so when I woke, I did not get dressed.

The doorbell went and I opened it, saying I had decided to give it a go, and hadn't dressed, and then I suddenly realized that the person I was talking to was not Rupert. This completely threw me and, actually, made the rest of the day

11

incredibly difficult for me. I still do not really know why it upset me so much, but I do remember it taking my breath away.

I had been told that a sound recordist would be coming, but I had completely forgotten the fact, and it was such a surprise to find this chap in front of me instead of Rupert. When Jimmy Blanche did speak to me, all he said was that he was the sound recordist. It felt like an eternity before I asked him in!

They filmed me that day, but I did not feel very happy. The crew filmed almost every room in the house, and I could not understand why this was necessary. I thought it was a gardening programme we were filming. They filmed me in my office, and I noticed they were filming photographs and poems on my wall. This made me angry. I could not see what it had to do with gardening.

This belief, that we were making a gardening programme of a similar nature to those that had been shown before, was the biggest problem for me. I did not understand what the film crew were trying to get, and why they were filming what they were. I did ask several times, and got comments like, 'It will provide a link', but at this stage that did not mean very much. I am too busy to watch much television, and what I had seen of gardening programmes left me wondering.

So it went on over the next few weeks. I was desperately waiting to be filmed doing proper gardening, but they did not seem to want this.

All they seemed to want were my feelings and emotions. I felt very vulnerable and not very happy at this stage. Was it a gardening programme at all?

As the weeks went by it dawned on me that it

was actually me they wanted, and, at times, it felt like my very soul. They had started asking me questions about my background, where had I been brought up, where had I gone to school, and college etc.? I was not at all happy with this.

∗

They had started looking at things in my home— my CDs, books, photographs—and everything else, it seemed. I felt they were taking away what I loved, and what was mine and private to me. I was beginning to feel very trapped.

In order to facilitate filming, I was being told that I could not do this, or that, in my own home and garden—usually because conditions weren't right or they weren't ready to film—and this was getting me down. I told Rupert that gardens, and the plants in them, do not stop growing in order to wait for a camera crew.

7 July. I phoned Rupert in the morning in a very upset and emotional state. I asked him not to come as I did not feel that I could continue with the filming. I was extremely upset, and was crying. I felt I had been manipulated into this situation and it was not a gardening programme at all: it was about a person. If I had realized this in the very beginning, I doubt if I would have agreed to be involved.

Rupert suggested we meet in a pub for a late lunch and to talk things over. When I got there, it was very obvious that the crew thought it was something they had done and they all felt very hurt.

I explained that I did not think it was them, just the situation that I had been put in. Rupert said they were really trying to be my friends. I told them

13

I was a private person, and it was very difficult for me to go from spending most of my life coping on my own, to suddenly sharing my emotions with three people I hardly knew - and, when the series is shown, the viewers.

I am still a private person. At times I did not feel Rupert was listening to me. He would just continue to film, or he would say, 'We will come back to that at a later date.' I was not sure about which bit of 'No' he did not understand.

Jimmy explained that the series was high profile and that it would now have to be shown, as too much had been invested in it by this stage. Rupert added, if we could not work together, Nick would pull the team and put another one in its place. They were going to make a programme whatever. I said to myself, 'That's what they think!'

I knew all along that they would only get a programme if I wanted it. No one, not even the BBC, could get me to do something if I did not want to do it, and being told that they thought they could only made me feel even angrier. I did say that I was not sure if I wanted to continue.

After a very long chat, we left the pub and Rupert said he would come to see me in the morning. During the evening I wondered about the legal implications if I refused to continue. I had no one to talk to about this situation and felt very isolated.

I did not know anyone, personally, who also worked in television, that I felt I knew well enough to pick up the phone and talk to about how I was feeling. You cannot just phone Alan Titchmarsh and chat to him, but I felt it was someone like him that I needed to talk to. I eventually went to bed feeling very miserable, unsure about everything.

The following morning Rupert did call, and we chatted. We decided that he would give me more time and we wouldn't try to do too much filming in one go. We had been filming four days at a time, and this was disrupting my life too much as I had lots of other work that I was trying to do too. I was not coping well with my emotions, which were all over the place. I had never experienced these feelings before and felt very uncertain.

Rupert explained that the programme was about gardening but looking through one person's eyes, and they wanted to show my love and passion. He said that he had seen things that he had never thought would have a place in a horticulturist's life. People would be interested in this. I just could not see why anyone would want to watch me in my home with my neighbours doing what I do on a day-to-day basis!

Over the next few months, through to the end of October, we developed a technique of filming and working together, and my trust in the team developed into what is now a very special relationship. We also had great fun together and enjoyed many funny experiences.

On the first occasion that we filmed at Writtle College, where I lecture part-time in horticulture, Jimmy, the sound recordist, made his own way there. Rupert travelled with me, and Kate followed in the crew car.

When we arrived in the car park I saw that Jimmy's car was already there and parked near to it. Rupert and I got out, and as we walked over to Jimmy's car I noticed that he was having 40 winks. I went up to the car, opened the driver's door very quietly, and shouted 'Boo!' Jimmy shot out of his seat with arms flailing everywhere. Rather unkindly, I just dissolved into a heap of laughter, tears rolling down my face. Rupert looked on, somewhat surprised!

When Jimmy calmed down and got his composure together, he looked at me and said that revenge was sweet, and to watch out.

We had been filming for a while when Rupert decided that he would take Jimmy and me into a wheatfield to do some filming. He asked Kate to stay at the college with the crew car. After about two hours, Rupert realized that Kate was still at the college, so he asked Jimmy just to let her know what we were up to.

Jimmy rang Kate on his mobile, but chose to tell her that I had been involved in a car accident and had written off my car. As I had been speeding, the police were taking particulars, so we could not get back to her. Poor old Kate was most concerned and said she would come, but Jimmy told her not to as a police officer was approaching the car. At that moment she saw us arriving and she realized she had been wound up—and was not very happy about this.

I said that I was not very happy about Rupert and Jimmy filming me in the field having a pee! Kate instantly started telling Rupert off about this, so I walked up to her, held out my hand and said, 'This sort of pea.' Opposite the wheat was a field of peas, which I had been helping myself to. I just love eating raw peas.

I think we all saw in each other a shared sense of fun and mischief, which showed itself on more than one occasion during the making of Series One.

I had another difficult emotion to handle at this time, and that was a feeling of emptiness after a day's filming. I often felt drained and very tired after filming, but did not have anything to show for the day's work. The film crew had the tape, but in spite of having worked hard all day I had nothing at all to see. Normally, I can see what I have achieved at the end of a day. I had never known a summer in which I'd felt so empty and lacking in job satisfaction.

I did not get to see a single shot of myself on film until Rupert and I started to do the voice-overs in November. This was a deliberate decision by the team. They did not want me to see myself in case I did not like what I saw, and changed my actions.

This left me wondering if it was all OK. What did I look like? Was it good enough to be shown on air? What did I sound like? What had I said (as nothing was scripted it was all spontaneous)? Was it technically correct? What did my garden look like? How had they put the programme together? It was a very strange feeling and, again, left me feeling very insecure and apprehensive.

I did not know, even now, if I could do television, and not seeing what I had done made me anxious. I just kept saying to myself that they would not keep filming if it was rubbish.

Eventually, on 8 November, I went up to BBC Mailbox in Birmingham to do my first voice-over and saw my first shots of *Christine's Garden*. I was moved to tears. It was really nice. My garden and home looked great. It was hard to believe it was my home, my garden and me. I saw the opening shots and could not believe it.

The music Rupert had selected fitted the shots fantastically. We had talked about my love of music, and he knew I was very keen on classical music. He had let slip, a few weeks previously, that he was looking at jazz and I felt very unhappy about that. I did not have any say in the matter, of course, and had been concerned that it would not really fit in with my lifestyle and the content of the programme. But it was lovely, and appropriate to the things that were being shown.

Neither Rupert, nor anyone else, had played about with the film much, and it showed Christine as Christine really is. It was my life, me and what I do. The shots of other people looked great, too. I was so very relieved.

Driving home, I had to get off the motorway as I kept crying, recalling what had been shown to me. I found it extremely difficult to concentrate, and felt as if a great burden had been lifted off my back. For the first time since that phone call, way back in January, I felt everything was fine.

During November and December, I made various trips to Birmingham to complete the voice-overs. Everyone at the BBC, without exception, was lovely to me, and, it became very apparent that they were all working so hard to make *Christine's Garden* as good as it could be. The team were extremely talented, true professionals, and I felt very humbled at being allowed to work with such gifted people.

The year had not been an easy one for me. I had to come to terms with three people being in my home, and garden, on a regular basis. What it taught me was that programme-making is a team effort and every member contributes. I was only a very tiny part of the whole thing. I felt I was the hub in the middle of a bicycle wheel, while the real talent lay in all the spokes that held the wheel together.

The three people that I had spent most of the year with had become very special to me. They had learnt a lot about me and my life. I know I am not the easiest person in the world. They had been very tolerant, understanding, patient, loving and professional.

I was still feeling apprehensive. I had been given a transmission date and I would be away for the first showing of Programme One. What would people think? What would my fellow professionals say? I was very worried about this. What affect would it have on my working life? I felt I would have liked a much higher technical content, but the BBC did not want this. What would my family and friends think?

I spent the early part of Christmas Day with Reg and Pat, and then joined Louise and her family for the rest of the day. The following morning I went to Heathrow and flew out to India. I knew I needed to get away. I was emotionally, and physically, very tired. I wanted to be out in the wilds. I was going to try and see tigers.

JANUARY

1–4 January

I was on holiday in India enjoying game drives to see wild tigers (we saw two at close range). I love seeing plants and animals, wild and free. Even though these tigers were in a reserve, they still took a considerable amount of finding.

I was glad to be away from home in a wild environment, which I so enjoy. The sound of cicadas, the smiling faces of the people, the food and smells all transported me away from a year that had been emotionally charged and, at times, difficult to handle.

I was wondering what people thought about *Christine's Garden* (the first programme was shown on 30 December 2005), but I did not feel like making a phone call home to find out. When I am away I prefer to be out of contact with everyone. It is my time to replenish myself, and I like the solitude that this brings.

*

5–8 January

I returned home to lots of recorded phone messages, cards and e-mails. I did not understand what was happening to my e-mails, as the number I was receiving kept increasing. I thought there was something wrong with the machine until, eventually, at 623, they stopped.

The vast majority of these were from the general public who were commenting in a very positive, and complimentary, way about the programme. Some were long and very touching and I felt that they needed a reply. Over the past few days, I've spent most of my time trying to reply to them.

What I have not realized is the enormity of the task ahead of me. Every time I've turned on my computer recently, comments and praise have flooded in. The BBC decided to do a direct link from the BBC gardening website to mine, and this has directed e-mails my way.

I have been finding it very difficult to get back into the swing of things. The phone has kept ringing, the letters have arrived and the e-mails, by the end of this week, have got to nearly 800! I'd had no idea what to expect, but this is something that I really hadn't thought about. Various members of the press contacted me to carry out interviews for the local papers.

I watched a video recording of my first programme at Reg and Pat's. They were very happy with it, but, in an odd way, I felt flat. I did not know why, but I felt nothing at all. I felt it was neither good nor bad; I was not concerned about what I had said or looked like. I found it very difficult to understand that it was me. It did not feel like me, it was almost like watching someone else.

＊

9–15 January

I returned to teaching this week and my students were very excited about the programme, and said very complimentary things. I had great difficulty getting them to stop asking questions, and I felt very guilty chatting to them about it when I was supposed to be teaching them! All that week the students only wanted to talk about the series and what was happening to me.

The e-mails continued to flood in, along with more cards and letters. I was now beginning to get emotional about the comments and praise. I suppose what I was actually feeling was relief that it was OK, and people did like it. It was the number that kept coming that I found difficult. I had expected friends to comment but had no idea that the public would respond in the way they did.

I drove up to my parents in Rishton, near Blackburn, and showed them the e-mails etc. They said they were very proud of me.

I had been invited by BBC Radio Lancashire to be a guest on a programme in the style of *Desert Island Discs* called *My Top Ten*, and had selected my ten favourite pieces of music that reflected my life and experiences.

These are the pieces of music that I included:

'Emerald Dew' and 'Winter Sun'—both
performed by The Fivepenny Piece
This group was very popular while I was in my
first job, and when I went to the Lancashire
College of Agriculture. The words they wrote
for a lot of their songs are very beautiful, and
create mental pictures of Lancashire and the
Lancastrian way of life. They often performed
at King George's Hall, which was just up the
road from Northgate, where my parents had
their shop—W.A. Walkden Sports Ltd.

'Fernando'—Abba
This takes me back to my first sandwich work
placement from college at The Luddington

Experimental Horticultural Station in Warwickshire. I worked with trees and shrubs, and had to propagate weeds for experiments on weed-killers and also take 10,000 gooseberry cuttings! The chap I was working with loved this song and would turn the radio up really loud each time it was on.

'Perhaps Love' (vocal duet)—John Denver and Placido Domingo
I think that both of these performers bring a sensitivity to a song that gives greater depth and meaning as it reflects their feelings on love and life. I like it so much because of the words, and its reflective quality.

'Romance' from *The Gadfly*—Shostakovich
This is a piece of music that I have enjoyed for many years and always takes me back to the movement of a wheat field in the wind. I close my eyes and just watch the wheat ripple and dance on a warm summer's day with bright blue skies.

'Canon in D'—Pachelbel
I have enjoyed this piece of music for a long time, but I will never forget one occasion when I was in a monastic garden in Santiago de Compostela and it was being played on the organ. To me, it perfectly fitted the place, the warmth of the day and the serenity created in such a beautiful Spanish garden. I was leading a garden tour, and it made the visit to this small garden very special. Every time I hear it now I am back in Spain.

'Lara's Theme' from *Doctor Zhivago*—
Maurice Jarre
How well this conjures up Russia, the very
beautiful scenery, birch and poplar trees and
the great times I have had on tours looking at
plants in the wild. Russia is full of magic,
fantastic buildings, great music and lovely
plants.

'Judex'—Gounod
For me this brings back memories of vast open
spaces, a sense of freedom and the wind.

'Dances with Wolves'—John Barry
This music reminds me of the very special
relationship which can develop between man
and animals. As a family we have always had
dogs and they have all come from rescue
centres. My second dog, Tara, is 14 years old
and very special to me.

'Teaching Andrea' from *Ladies in Lavender*—
Nigel Hess
This piece of music was the one I listened to
most after a day's filming for *Christine's
Garden* during last year. A relatively new
piece, written for the film, which I have still
not seen, it relaxes me and I love the phrasing.

'What a Wonderful World'—Louis Armstrong
This is the last piece of music that you hear on
the final programme of *Christine's Garden* in
series one, and sums up my views on life and
last year's experiences.

I was beginning to feel shattered by all that was going on and was finding things very difficult. I have no idea why, looking back, but I kept crying at the slightest bit of praise. People kept stopping me when I was out and would express nice comments to me and said some lovely things about Reg, Louise and Tara. I thought I would not be able to handle being approached, but, actually, found it easier than I had anticipated.

I went to Broadcasting House to give an interview on the *Johnny Walker Drive Time Show* on Radio 2. This went well and again people were nice about the series. As I walked out of the studio, the producer handed me a copy of the e-mails that they had received while I was on the air. Yet again, they commented on my joy, enthusiasm and love of gardening.

The following morning I was in London again to give another radio interview, this time for Radio 4 *Woman's Hour*. When I got home a friend phoned and said to read the e-mail she had just sent me. It commented on the interview: 'This was super—she thought you were going to talk about potatoes but you talked about the soul. This interview encapsulated the whole of your philosophy and the meaning of the garden—plants—and your television programme. It was superb!! Very well done.' I had not had praise like this ever before.

*

16–22 January
The e-mails kept on flooding in after every programme shown. By now they numbered over 1,000, saying really very nice things, but I was

struggling to keep on top of them and was feeling totally overwhelmed.

I spoke to my brother, who is good with computers, and he suggested that I could probably do a blanket 'thank-you' to most of the e-mails, but, although I did not like doing this, I was not coping at all and was getting upset by my inability to type quickly enough. It mattered to me that I should reply to most of the e-mails. It was obvious that people had spent ages writing and the idea of sending them a standard reply grated like mad, but in the end I had no option. In some ways I'm beginning to dread Friday evenings.

My students continued to comment in a very positive manner and even the estate maintenance and administrative staff at Writtle College had become great fans of the programme. I was very touched by this. However, only two of my fellow lecturers made any comment at all.

Newspapers were approaching me for interviews, and the *Lancashire Evening Telegraph* wanted to follow up the radio interview I had given on BBC Lancashire in *My Top Ten*. To say I was busy was a great understatement.

I went round to Reg and Pat's to see programme four. This was about returning to Lancashire, my old allotment and college life. This was the first programme I felt I could relate to. It was filmed so very beautifully and the music captured the feelings so well. Rupert had done a great job with this and, once again, the e-mails came in, but this time, in the main, they were from Lancastrians. They loved what Rupert had shown and the feedback was very positive. I felt so very proud of what Rupert had filmed. To me this will always be the programme I remember best from series one.

✳

23–31 January
I spent most of the week clearing all the e-mails that still kept coming in. I had now dealt with over 1,500 and was still finding that every time I turned on my computer there were more.

These were all really very nice but I was getting very tired of all the typing. I am only a 'two-finger typist' and I was spending most of my time on the computer, which I cannot say I greatly enjoy. My only consolation was that the weather was very cold and working outside for any period of time was not pleasant.

FEBRUARY

1–7 February

I was asked to do an interview on BBC breakfast television about the growing numbers of women who take on allotment sites. A car collected me, at 5 a.m., and took me to Television Centre in London. I was brought home by 10.30 a.m.

This was just a short interview, but the number of phone calls and e-mails on my return showed how many people watch TV in the morning. I don't myself, because I am too busy getting breakfast, walking Tara and organizing my day.

I lectured at Writtle College during the week, and my students continued to take a great interest in *Christine's Garden*. They were pleased that my activities with them, at the college, had been featured, and they felt the students, college and I came across very well.

The weather continued to be bitterly cold and, at this time of the year, I would normally be turning over the vegetable garden, but I felt it was better to leave it a while until the weather improved.

I went round to see Regand Pat, and we watched the final programme in the series together. They both seemed very pleased with how the series had gone, and were now regularly being stopped, when out shopping, by people asking for their autograph, or commenting on the series and asking when we would be making another.

In my opinion Reg has become a 'star'. People ask about him everywhere I go.

They do not always remember his name, but ask about the chap with the smile. I know who they mean!

Immediately after the programme had finished, I did a web chat on the BBC's gardening message board, and was very surprised at the level of interest. By the end of the evening, the site had over 450 hits. This not only surprised me, but also the BBC co-ordinator, when I eventually phoned her at 11 p.m. She said they were not expecting so much activity, and, even when I had logged off, the e-mails continued.

Being a slow typist I answered as many e-mails as I could, but, after two hours, was shattered and felt I had done my bit. The BBC had expected me to run for an hour, so I felt I had been fair with everyone. There was no way I was going to be able to answer them all.

I try to attend to the incoming e-mails on my own website, but find it hard to keep up with them. Surely it can't go on much longer. Now that the series is over, the e-mails should stop. How wrong can you be? In practice I can imagine that they'll carry on coming right throughout the year.

During the week I presented a 'How to sell' course for a local training group of the Horticultural Trades Association. I enjoy these courses very much. By questioning their techniques I try to help people realize their potential.

The course contains a number of exercises where the candidates have to sell something, first to each other and then to me. In the end they enjoy this part of the course, but they usually start nervously. I test them at first with some item they know well, and then with a product they have never sold. This exercise makes them identify all the different skills you need for selling. I am not the easiest customer, as I hate shopping, so the exercise is very realistic. I can be, when I have to, one of the most difficult customers they will ever come across!

*

8–12 February

I went to North Wales for a few days with a friend to do some hill-walking and visit some gardens. We both made it up Snowdon, on a grey and cold day, but could not see a thing at the top. We had been engulfed in mist for the final hour of our climb.

I always enjoy the rather fantastical village of Portmeirion, not just for the fascinating blend of architecture that Sir Clough Williams-Ellis put together, but also for the lovely wild walks around the coast and estate. Paths follow the coast for a reasonable distance and then criss-cross through sub-tropical woodland before returning to the village, and the many visitors.

Plas Brondanw, where Sir Clough Williams-Ellis lived, is not far away, and I enjoy visiting his garden. I reflect on the romance, and sense of drama, that he created using hedging and topiary, and his careful framing, within the garden, of the majestic view of Snowdon.

I love mountains, and when I can see gardens, mountains and open spaces together I am in my element!

The following day we went on to the Great Orme

at Llandudno, looked at the promontory's vegetation and birds, before returning to our accommodation in Beddgelert and going out to an excellent local bistro for a lovely meal.

*

13–19 February
I spent this week mainly completing consultancies around Essex and Bedfordshire, when I was not at college, lecturing to my RHS (Royal Horticultural Society) Level 2 and RHS Advanced Certificate students.

These consultancies varied. In the first one my job was to identify a drainage problem. Moss was growing on the lawn and plants were dying, especially in the low spots of the garden. Drains had already been installed in the garden, but it turned out that the water was not draining into the pipes, as these had not been installed according to the specification. The only solution was to get the contractors back to sort out the problem and in the meantime only to plant on a mound and add plenty of sharp grit into the planting compost.

In the second consultancy a conifer hedge was going yellow and dying from the middle, and slowly this damage was progressing along the hedge in either direction. It had been doing this for the past 18 months. A close inspection of the soil around the base of the hedge, and the stems of the plants, showed this to be caused by honey fungus. Unfortunately, there is not a lot that can be done, at this stage, other than to suggest removing the hedge completely along with the root system and erecting a fence. Fortunately, a fence would be an acceptable option on this occasion.

31

Another consultancy visit had me thinking about the practical problems of trying to rectify a change in soil acidity due to a large amount of dog urine. The people I had gone to see had kennels, and found that nothing would grow in the courtyard area where the dogs were exercised every day. They wanted to try and establish a lawn.

I did explain that, for the size of plot, there were too many dogs for grass to grow well, as the constant trampling would wear the grass away. I then tested the soil, only to find that it was very acid, and would need the application of a lot of lime to rectify the problem. It would probably also take 18–24 months to get the soil into a state to allow a lawn to establish. Luckily a large field was available, and an easier option was to exercise the dogs in this much bigger area rather than in the courtyard.

Another aspect of my week's work was to respond to a phone call from someone who wanted my opinion on his ability to sit the RHS Level 2 examination this year. I met him, and went through various sections of the syllabus. Unfortunately, I concluded that he did not have sufficiently wide-ranging knowledge to be sure of success.

This examination requires a good general level of knowledge of the practice of gardening, as well as the science behind it, and this chap just did not have the information, especially in the sciences, to make me feel confident. I advised him to consider a college course to bring him up to speed on the sciences before he attempted the examination. I could see he was disappointed by this, but he took it very well and thanked me for my time and patience.

I had recently been approached by various magazines to write weekly articles for them, so I wrote a few trial pieces. Both *Amateur Gardening* and *Garden News* commissioned me to write regularly, initially for a period of three months.

From what I can gather, this three-month trial period gives the editor a chance to see if you can produce suitable articles and deliver them on time. Weekly newspapers and magazines sail close to the wind with their production schedules, so copy deadlines are very important, as is the ability to deliver the correct number of words and, in some cases, photographs to go with the article.

20–24 February

Tara was worrying me as she was not eating much and her back legs seemed to be giving way. She is now getting old but I hope she will live a bit longer. I had to carry her outside, as she was having difficulty getting over the back doorstep. Once I got her going she seemed reasonable, but when she had been lying down she found it difficult to start walking.

After a couple of days, I took Tara to the vet, who examined her and said he thought a past hip injury was causing her pain and this had put her off eating. He gave her an injection, and prescribed some tablets for me to give her over the next two weeks, saying he thought she would be fine when she had finished them. To my relief, this turned out to be correct.

I went to see a local garden that had got overgrown, and spent the next three days pruning apple trees and shrubs, in an attempt to get some vigour back into them, and to improve the overall visual impact of the garden. Some of the shrubs had not been pruned in years and needed substantial rejuvenating pruning, which basically involves pruning the shrubs down to about 30cm (1 foot) high.

I think the lady who owned the garden was amazed at what I had achieved in three days. Afterwards she said that she had thought I was going to recommend taking everything out and starting again!

> *In some circumstances, this may be the way forward, but, if you remove established shrubs, you are removing age and character. I would only recommend complete removal if the plant was diseased, damaged or dead, or was causing some other major problem.*

It wasn't just my RHS students who were commenting on *Christine's Garden*. A farmers' market course which I was presenting started late as I could not stop the trainees discussing the programme. I find this sort of situation difficult to handle. I feel I should be carrying out the training and asking them to save the chat until break time, but, inevitably, something crops up which makes them comment during a session. I am very flattered by the interest, but cannot help wondering what the organization would think, if they were to sit in on a session. Having said that, at one place where I turned up to carry out some training they actually encouraged me to share my experiences with the group. However, I do not feel it is very professional.

I also find it embarrassing, as do not see myself as a TV celebrity. I feel that celebrity status should be reserved for professionals who have served their time by working in television for years, and know all the ins and outs of making programmes. To me, it is people like Dame Judi Dench and Sir John Gielgud who are celebrities. Not me, who has just popped up and done six programmes. I find it odd how appearing once or twice on television can change the way people view you. I am just the same as I was before doing the series, so cannot understand what all the fuss is about.

I went into BBC Essex to carry out my regular live two-hour phone-in session and it was completely taken over by people asking me about the series and commenting on the programmes. The presenter didn't seem to mind and was actually encouraging listeners to phone in and comment.

What I have found very surprising is that I, personally, have not had one even slightly derogatory comment expressed to me. Only nice ones came to my website—I had received over 2,000 e-mails by this stage. However, there were some odd, cranky and slightly offensive ones put up on the BBC website message boards. Several had a go at my personal appearance, saying I was fat, ugly and needed a stylist. Well, this just amused me, but did cause offence to several of my close friends.

Vanity is not something I am even aware of. I have lived with me and my appearance for some time now and know that at 5 foot 1 inch, I am rather small, tend to be well-built, but not obese as was suggested more than once, and will never win a beauty competition. They would have to try much harder if they were trying to have a go at me.

What did come across very strongly to me was the vast amount of pleasure the series had given. At the beginning, I was not sure people would even watch it. I did not anticipate this appreciation at all and found all the e-mails to me to be very touching.

Looking back, I am glad I had the courage to say yes, as I very nearly didn't. I learned a lot about myself, some of which has been painful. For the first time in my whole career, I had to think about the full picture—past colleagues, friends, clients, students and others. I was, and am, always more interested in what I have to do for tomorrow instead of giving any time to what had happened in the past.

I have kept hundreds of the e-mails in a file, as I still do not really believe all this has happened to me. In many ways it does not feel real. I cannot believe that my first series has come and gone, and people are still e-mailing me and talking about it when they meet me.

I find it fascinating that people watched a normal person doing her normal work in a normal manner, and responded in the way they did. I feel honoured, and very privileged, to have been given the opportunity to communicate a love affair with plants, one that means the world to me.

What I did not realize was that I had shared this love affair before, and it had changed people. I enjoy what I do and that's where it begins and ends. I do not think that previously I had ever thought beyond that. The series brought home to me how much I must have affected many people. I had just never seen it before.

MARCH

1 March

The weather is very cold at the moment and nothing much is happening in the garden.

I spent the morning writing my weekly articles for *Garden News* and *Amateur Gardening*. I am used to writing, so a weekly deadline is not a worry for me, and, fortunately, they have asked me to write on very different subjects. The *Garden News* piece is about what I am doing at the moment in my life and in my garden, on both professional and amateur levels; while *Amateur Gardening* have asked me to write and comment on topical issues.

In the evening I had my final class with my RHS General Certificate students, who have been with me for five terms. This is the final year in which students will be taking this examination in March. The new syllabus gives them the option of a February or July examination date.

I find the last evening of any course difficult. Over five terms you get to know your students— they have become friends—and you also understand how it feels to be approaching an exam. Several of them have not taken an examination in many years, and their apprehension shows. All I can do is reassure them and give them as much help as possible.

On these occasions I often feel very emotional on my way home in the car. It's the thought that you have no idea how they will do in the examination, and what they will go on to achieve. I also find it sad that I may never see some of these people again. Such is life. What has become apparent, through the many e-mails and letters I have had following the showing of *Christine's Garden*, is that a lot of them remember me very fondly. I have had e-mails from some students that I taught over 30 years ago. That is very nice and makes you realize that all your efforts are appreciated.

Most of my groups give me a 'thank-you' card and, sometimes, a present at the end of the course. It's the cards that mean the most to me, as they often contain some lovely words of thanks, and, at the end of the day, it is these words that make it so worthwhile. I am a softy, and I keep them carefully. Occasionally I will get them out and reflect on the names, and then I find myself wondering what the people are doing now.

✽

2 March

I drove to Maidstone, in Kent, to carry out a consultancy for a lady who had a small garden and was unsure what to do with it, and what plants would be suitable.

> *Many people whom I visit have great ideas, but just need reassurance that what they would like to do is viable.*

This lady had some good ideas, too, but was at a loss about what to plant in the shade at the front of her house. The area is small and narrow, and the beds are not very big. I asked her if she would send me accurate measurements of the areas for which she wanted plans.

I enjoy providing planting plans; this is where I feel I utilize most of my experience and knowledge. I am not keen on surveying a site and drawing up a plan, as I find this to be the boring bit. What I do enjoy is putting plants together to meet a client's needs.

It's surprising the factors you have to think about—soil conditions and aspect of the site, seasonality and availability of water. You also need to form an understanding of the owners themselves—how much money do they want to spend? What sort of an atmosphere do they wish to create? And are they going to be doing the planting and maintenance themselves, or will they be getting someone else to do it for them?

✱

3 March
I decided to take a few photographs to illustrate some articles I had written. The main article was about how, at this time of the year, I take new cuttings from young plants which were themselves grown from cuttings last August and over-wintered on my windowsill. These had originally been an insurance policy in case frost killed off the mother plants left outside.

I usually take cuttings any time between August and October.

I have limited growing space inside my house, and cannot possibly bring all my non-hardy plants in for the winter. My house is fairly full already with well over 200 houseplants. By taking cuttings in the autumn, I have a back-up in case the main plant dies. What I find is that these young plants grow quickly in the spring and I am able to take three or four more cuttings from them and bulk up my plants that way.

To take cuttings, all I do is take about 5-8cm (2-3 inches) of the growing point from the plant, strip off the lower leaves and then place these cuttings around the edge of an 8cm (3-inch) plant pot full of multipurpose seed and cutting compost. This is placed back on the windowsill. Sometimes, if the cuttings wilt, I will put a clear plastic bag over the top of them to try and increase the humidity, but this is not normally needed at this time of the year.

✳

4–5 March

I spent some of the weekend digging over my vegetable plot. This involved taking out a trench, half-filling it with partially rotted leafmould from leaves collected last autumn, then filling it in again with the soil taken by digging out the next trench, and so on across the plot.

The autumn leaves that are used to fill the trenches are collected up into black dustbin bags, into which I pour a gallon of water—even if they are damp, they still need extra moisture. I then tie the neck of the bag and, finally, put a few holes in the side for drainage. The bags are placed behind the compost bins, at the top of the garden, until I need them. Often the leaves are not really fully broken down when I use them, but this doesn't worry me: on my very light soil, provided the leaves are damp, they rot very quickly once covered by soil.

When I am digging over my plot I put into the trenches as much organic matter as I can—in the way of leaves, kitchen waste, old compost, rotted manure and just about anything I can get hold of. I add all this organic matter because it acts like a sponge in the summer, and helps to retain moisture at root level where the plants need it.

In the case of a heavy soil, the material should be composted first.

In the autumn I cover much of the vegetable plot with a green manure crop to protect the surface of the soil, and help retain all the plant nutrients, which otherwise can get washed away by winter rains. This past autumn I sowed a mixed green manure, containing silage grains, at a rate of about 50g per sq m (roughly 2 oz per sq yard).

Because my soil is light, I never dig in the autumn, as this would cause it to be compacted by winter rains, and it would need re-cultivating in the spring.

During the morning, I met up with an old friend and we went to the Early Spring Show of the Alpine Garden Society (AGS) in Harlow. I have always had a keen interest in alpines and, for some years, was the secretary of this show, so I am always interested in attending, if work and time allow.

This is the AGS's first show of the year, and I always think it's one of the best. That's probably due to the number of bulbs that are shown in flower, but it is also just so pleasing to see good plants again after the winter. I am always amazed at the colour and variety of the plants, and their high quality, at this time of year.

Today's visit was very different from other years, as lots and lots of people stopped me to congratulate me on my first series. This, initially, was fine, and people were saying extremely nice and positive things, but it meant that I was unable to spend much time looking at, and enjoying, the plants. In the end I gave up trying and decided that I should just chat to people. Then I started to appreciate what was being said, instead of being frustrated that I could not look around.

In the early evening I took Tara round to Reg and Pat's so they could look after her while I drove up to Lancashire to stay overnight with my parents in Rishton, near Blackburn. I arrived at their home after midnight, feeling very tired.

6 March

I was at Writtle College all day with my RHS Monday group, completing practical work. We were looking at outdoor seed-bed preparation.

First I gave a demonstration. It involved forking over the ground to relieve the winter compaction.

The soil is opened up by pushing the tines of the fork about 8cm (3 inches) into it. You do not need to turn the soil over, as this brings weed seeds to the surface, resulting in more work once the crop has come through the soil.

The next job was to rake the soil to produce the

correct particle size in relation to the size of seed being sown. This is a highly skilled job and one that students find very difficult to achieve. First they have to rake the ground, then gently firm it, using the balls of the feet, to ensure that the particles are in contact with each other, leaving enough air still present in the soil.

It sounds very easy to rake a piece of land and get it level, but in practice, until you have had enough experience of the job, you normally end up with a saucer shape and a rim of stones and soil around the edge of the plot. When I carry out the demonstration, I get it right first time, and it causes the students a lot of frustration! I try to explain that they are seeing the result of years of practice, and the only way they are going to produce the right result is to do the same.

It can take a couple of hours before everyone in the group is at a standard to be able to move on to the next stage, which is seed sowing.

For this you use a hoe to take out a long, straight depression in the soil. The easiest hoe to use is a draw hoe. First you put down a garden line, as a guide, so that the depression is straight; you then pull the corner of the hoe through the soil to make a channel into which the seeds can be sown. You always need to judge the depth depending on the size of the seed. I always follow the instructions on the packet. If the channel is too shallow, not enough soil will cover the seeds and they will dry out; if it's too deep, the seeds will run out of food before getting through to the light, and will just die.

Again, this can take time, as the channel needs to be level so that all the seeds grow at the same rate. Commercially, we are after consistency of growth, at all stages, so that all the jobs can be done in one go. Variation in growth means going through the crop several times to complete each job.

We then moved on to the actual sowing, first with very small seeds, such as lobelia; then medium-sized seeds, such as cabbage, and, finally, large seeds such as peas or beans, to show the students the different techniques that are used.

Students often start out thinking that sowing is one of the simpler gardening jobs to carry out. After I've spent a day with them they are far more aware that every single aspect of gardening, at a professional level, is highly skilled. You cannot get away with working to the less exacting standards of an amateur.

Those students who find this difficult to understand can also find me a difficult taskmaster, as I will not compromise on standards. I believe it should be obvious from the work that you produce that you are a professional, and you should take a pride in what you do. After some time they normally come round to my way of thinking; after all, they are not going to be allowed to move forward until they do!

7 March

I spent the morning in north London carrying out a Horticultural Trades Association Retail Plant Care Award practical assessment on a candidate in Camden.

This is not an easy award to achieve, but one that carries with it a lot of respect if you can pass it. The assessment starts with me, as the assessor, asking questions on compulsory subjects such as Health and Safety issues. I then set the candidate a plant identification test and a pest, disease and weed identification test. He or she then moves on to questions based on irrigation and watering, quality control and the company's delivery procedure. The assessment takes place where the candidate works, and can take up to two hours to complete.

The candidate I was working with today gained a pass and seemed very pleased that he had achieved the necessary result. We both went off to inform his boss, who was also very happy.

During the afternoon Nick Patten, the Executive Producer of *Christine's Garden*, phoned me to tell me that the BBC had just commissioned another series. He congratulated me, and we discussed the possibility of having the same film crew as last time. He was hopeful, but said he would let me know. I explained that I had a special relationship with Rupert Miles, the director. In the first series he was not only the director but also the producer and cameraman. Nick said he was aware of the relationship that had developed during the making of the first series.

Once I put the phone down, I was extremely excited and felt, for the very first time, that I could actually do television. I know this will sound mad, but it's true. I had seen the first series go out, received over 2,500 e-mails all saying very nice things to me, and been sent hundreds of cards and letters; the viewing figures were good, and people at the BBC had said lovely things to me; people in the streets stopped me and letters had been published in gardening magazines all saying good things about the series, but when Nick said those few words—'A second series has been commissioned'—I felt so much relief. For the first time I had belief in myself, it was OK and I was moving forward.

The rest of the day was spent in a very odd mood. I had difficulty phoning people with my news. I do not know why, but, somehow, it felt like I was bragging, and that I shouldn't have been. The few people I did phone were very happy for me and congratulated me.

*

8 March

Rupert phoned me to have a chat about the new series, and what we might cover, and to congratulate me. I said that congratulations were due to him. After all, it was Rupert who made the series; I just gave the material. He was very happy. He would be working on the new series and we discussed getting together for a meeting up at the BBC in Birmingham next week.

I feel very privileged to have been involved in the making of a TV series. I now have a much greater understanding of what it takes, and of all the very hard work that is done by a vast team of people—not just the film crew but everyone back at Birmingham, from concept, through production, to going out on air.

I then went off to a farm shop in Buntingford, Hertfordshire, to give some advice on display and methods of increasing sales. It always surprises me how people take on a retail business with little idea of what is actually involved. However, if they stick at it and accept the very steep learning curve, and hours and hours of hard work, they normally come through and make a success of it all.

The owner of this shop had made the usual errors. Fruit and vegetables were stacked on the shelves without much thought given to presentation, prices were not clear, produce was mixed together in a very random fashion, items were not all clearly labelled and packing material was not always available.

I often say to business owners that they had to be taught how to drive a car, so what makes them think that they don't need a bit of help in learning how to run a business? All I do is give some instructions that help them to drive their business forward.

I find this a very rewarding job, as the results of my efforts are to be seen if the client takes on board the advice given. This is not always the case!

9 March
Another garden consultancy up towards Cambridge. The lady had a very large garden on a light, chalky soil, that lacked colour, but she also wanted it to be low maintenance.

One of the largest problem areas was a very big border, 24m (80 feet) long by 3.6m (12 feet) wide, containing a lot of shrubs and trees, that needed pruning back hard to rejuvenate them. Also, the border looked good in the spring but there was nothing in it for the rest of the year.

I was asked to produce a planting plan, with

some ideas for introducing more colours into the border. Once I had talked the whole project through, asking the lady what plants she liked, etc, I advised her that, due to the probability of a drought this summer which was forecast for this part of the country, it would be better to leave the project until October, as any planting would have to be watered to ensure that the plants established properly. It also appeared that there was no water nearby, and the thought of having to bring a hose pipe 200m (over 600 feet) across the garden, even if this was allowed, was too much. She agreed to have me back in October to carry out the necessary work.

10 March

I spent the day in the office sorting out e-mails and other paperwork.

I had a break in the middle of the day to go out to lunch with a gardening friend I have known for years, who wanted me to meet a 90-year-old friend of hers who had enjoyed *Christine's Garden* so much, she wanted to see me.

The 90-year-old lady was amazing. Such an enquiring mind, and what spirit! She asked me about how the series came about, what was involved, how it had affected me, had I enjoyed making it, and she was delighted when I invited her back to my house to see the garden for herself.

I very much enjoyed this break in the day. It was lovely seeing them both, and we had a nice, cooked lunch, which saved me getting a meal together in the evening.

I walked Tara down by the river, but the wind

was biting, and everything was still in tight bud, showing no movement towards growth at all. I would estimate that the season is behind by about three weeks. We did not go as far as we normally do, as it was so cold. Tara has arthritis and I am aware that, if she gets very cold, it plays havoc with her and she ends up in pain. So I cut the walk short and got her back into the warmth of the house.

I nipped round to Reg and Pat's in the evening to tell them that we had got a second series. Reg was so happy, it was really pleasing to see. He said he had done nothing and it was all down to me. I said that, for me, he was the real star of the first series and that, everywhere I go, people ask about him. He said he did not know why. I went on to tell him it was his lovely smile and manner that everyone appreciated, and that he did not have to do anything, as he was special just being himself. He roared with laughter.

One of the nicest things about the series, for me, was seeing how much Reg enjoyed being involved. He always smiles and is such a happy, contented chap; he always makes me smile and it was a delight having him join in. I realize now that I never formally asked Reg or Louise if they wanted to be involved in the series—it just happened. As they won't be paid, it's nice to know they're doing it because they want to help me.

I went round to see if Louise, my neighbour who lives next door but two, was in and, as she was, invited her round to join us. We celebrated with a bottle of wine and ate cheese and biscuits, and talked about who would be involved with the production. I told them that Rupert would be filming and directing, and I was hopeful that Jimmy and Kate would be involved. They all were very pleased with this news.

*

11–12 March

Despite the very cold weather I managed to get some more gardening done this weekend. I planted out some hellebore seedlings that I had grown from seed sown three years ago. These went in my north-facing border with plenty of compost placed in the planting hole.

I always water my plants the night before planting, and then water them after they are planted in their final positions.

The lawn had started to grow so I decided to give it the first cut of the season. I got out my mower, adjusted the height of cut to about 5cm (2 inches) and took just about a 2cm (0.75 inch) off. Over the season, I will gradually lower the height of cut to a final height of about 2.5cm (1 inch). I am not a great fan of closely mown grass, so I tend to leave my lawn with a more natural look.

I completed some more digging of the vegetable patch. The soil was a bit on the sticky side, so I put a plank down to work from. I didn't wish to cause damage to the soil surface by walking on it when it was sticky. This would destroy the surface particle structure, which would then take a number of years to re-form.

I have a great respect for soil. It is the gardener's life-blood. I get very offended when people call it dirt or mud, as this shows how little they understand about its magical ingredients.

I often tell my students that a teaspoonful of soil contains more organisms than the number of people living on this planet. Isn't that amazing? There are many other ingredients that make it so wonderful. I wish I had the ability to show gardeners just how it works and what it can do if you really look after it properly.

In the evening I got out all the notes and handouts I need for the week's lecturing at college. This always takes longer than I expect, as I have four groups on the go at any one time. I find it much easier teaching different subjects than the same subject four times a week.

*

13 March
I was in college all day. During the morning I taught the theoretical aspects of plant propagation, and in the afternoon I demonstrated to the group how to take softwood, semi-ripe and hardwood cuttings.

We discussed the different stages of growth. Softwood is new growth, produced from the plant's growing tip between March and June, which is soft and contains no hardening fibres. Semi-ripe growth is that which is produced from late June through to about late September and has fibres inside which result in a certain stiffness. I often describe the wood at this stage as giving a feeling of tension similar to the one that you get if you play with a paper clip and try to break it. Hardwood is growth that is produced by the plant between October and March, and is fairly self-explanatory: it is like a pencil and, if you try to break it, it will snap in half because the fibres inside the plant have become very stiff and hard.

We then went on to a practical session, where the students learned how to take the three different types of cuttings. Students really enjoy this practical. I think it's because they can see how easy it is to produce new plants in a very simple way.

I do point out that the plants we are using are all very easy to root and so do not require any additional action, or treatments, to get them to root. This is not the case with lots of other plants that they will learn about later in the course.

*

14 March

A photographer had arranged to spend the morning with me, taking shots that would be used to illustrate my weekly contributions to *Amateur Gardening*. I find this process interesting. Although they will have given me a rough suggestion of topics to write about, the photographer and the editor have no idea what I am going to produce, so how do they know what photos they want before they receive my copy? Sometimes when I turn on the computer I haven't any idea either!

What normally occurs is that the photographer will get me to walk round my garden and he will take several shots, which always seem to be relevant in some way when they appear in the magazine; otherwise we nip off to a local garden centre, or exhibition garden, and take shots there.

In the afternoon I went to see a couple who have bought a very large garden full of trees and shrubs but do not know anything about looking after it. After a look round I suggested that, unless they were prepared to get someone in to look after the garden, it would deteriorate very quickly and this was a shame, as they had some lovely plants. They asked if I could suggest anyone, and I was able to pass on the names of two students who I felt would fit the bill.

In the evening I went over to Writtle College to lecture to my RHS Advanced Certificate students about plant physiology.

*

15 March
After a day spent in the office, preparing lecture notes and training material for courses that are coming up over the next few weeks, I set off at 5 p.m. to drive up to see friends in Birmingham for the night. Doreen had made a very nice meal for me, but, unfortunately, I missed the turning off the M6 and had a very difficult time getting back to her house. It didn't help that when I spoke to Doreen on the phone, she thought I was somewhere other than where I actually was, and gave me instructions to find her home from where she thought I was. This became apparent to me when I went past Edgbaston cricket ground for the third time! I eventually found her house at 9 p.m.

*

16 March
I drove into Birmingham for a meeting at the BBC

with everyone involved with the making of *Christine's Garden*.

I met some of the people who had been involved with the commissioning and production of the first series, and was given their congratulations on getting a further series, plus a lovely tied bouquet of flowers. This brought back memories of the first series, as I was sent flowers then. I love receiving flowers.

It was really a brainstorming session, in which all involved had the opportunity to have their say about what had worked well in the first series, what was worth trying to retain, what was needed to make the second series successful and what we should try to achieve.

I had not been involved with the initial discussions for the first series, so it was interesting for me to hear people's thoughts about a second series. What became apparent is that it is difficult to try to plan to film my life when I have no idea, from month to month, what I will be doing. What I do know is that if something is suggested that I would not normally do, in my garden or elsewhere, I am unhappy about the suggestion.

Good news followed: the previous soundman, Jimmy Blanche, had agreed to work on the second series. Unfortunately, however, Kate Hollingsworth, the assistant producer for the first series, had already moved on to a new production and would not be joining us. This disappointed me, as I like Kate very much. She made a large contribution to the series and is a thoughtful, caring person. However, for the sake of her own development, it's right that she should move on.

After the formal meeting, Rupert and I had a

chat about what we felt, and we decided to continue talking at intervals over the next couple of weeks to see what we thought could be achieved.

I felt that the meeting had gone well, and was thrilled that Rupert and Jimmy would be working with me. Both men are very talented, and both had given so much to series one that I would have been disappointed if they could not have been involved.

I then had a three-hour drive back home and had to go straight to college for my RHS evening class. I lectured on glasshouse crop production, focusing on tomatoes and cucumbers. I found this hard work after a day's discussion about TV. My mind was full of what had been said during the day.

17 March

I spent more time up in the vegetable garden, digging in compost and emptying my compost bins. I have four: one that's made out of wooden slats, another two that are made out of plastic and are traffic cone in shape, and a fourth which is an enormous, six-sided plastic box. They all make great compost.

I have a bucket by the kitchen door, and all my peelings and anything organic, except cooked meat, is put in the bucket. When this is full I take it up to the compost bin and mix it in with the rest of the stuff in the bin. Sometimes, if it is dry, I will water it, but in the main I find enough moisture is generated from the material itself.

The real secret of compost making is to mix everything together and not to put things on the heap in layers.

In the evening I prepared material for a creative planting course that I was giving at Writtle College over the weekend.

*

18–19 March

I was lecturing and completing practical work all weekend at college. This was an enjoyable course, as I had a very small group and was able to speak to everyone about their own gardens and any problems they had.

Over the weekend we covered the secrets of success when growing plants in various positions, and how to arrange them imaginatively. The students looked at different shapes of trees and shrubs, and thought about how to use them and choose the best place for them in their own gardens. They were asked to look at different textures of foliage and the different growth habits that can be used to create interest and movement in the garden.

I then demonstrated how to go about planting exciting hanging baskets and containers. We went across to the garden centre and I set them a challenge to spend no more than £15 per basket or container. They had to select their own plants, then go back to the greenhouse and use the plants to plant up a container, or hanging basket, for themselves. This proved very popular and created a very lively discussion about the plants used and how you should think about colour and scale when planting baskets and containers.

The students also had great fun, and got their hands very dirty, while being shown how to find out the soil type in their own garden. Many of the students, who live in this area, think that they have clay soils and so treat them as such, often without great success. This is because a lot of them actually have a high percentage of silt, not clay, in their soils.

The technique involves rolling and kneading soil in your hands with a little water. The students had to learn to feel the different soils such as clay, silt, loam or sandy soil, so that they can work out what, they have themselves. Soils can vary a lot, even from one end of a village to the other. Armed with this information, we then looked at plants suitable for different soil types.

The final session was looking at, and testing, pH and the influence it has in the soil. A lot of the students know that it relates to the amount of calcium, but are not aware that the degree of acidity/ alkalinity can either release, or lock up, plant nutrients. They find this simple test fascinating, and once they have carried it out on their own sample of soil, go home with specific knowledge they can use. I enjoy weekend courses, as you have time to answer queries and make the course applicable to the students' own gardens and, thus, more meaningful for them. This is not always possible in classes when you are teaching to a set syllabus.

*

20 March

I took my RHS Monday group down to the RHS garden at Wisley to show them various features. We looked at rock gardens, alpine houses (specialized greenhouses with more ventilation) and how they are constructed, the growing method for certain vegetables, the difference between fruiting buds and growth buds on apple trees, and how this influences pruning techniques.

We also spent time looking at the displays in the greenhouses, concentrating on plants that the students should know how to grow and propagate.

A number of the students had never been to this garden before. They always find it fascinating, and come to understand why I am so pedantic about standards when lecturing to them. They see for themselves the standards which the RHS set. In some ways I feel I should begin their course with a visit to Wisley, and then bring them back again towards the end of it, but, unfortunately, time does not allow this.

✳

21 March

I spent the morning in my office, and in the afternoon I went round to see how Reg's tomatoes were doing and to take a photograph of him with them for an article I had just written. We don't half tease each other about our tomatoes. His plants are already about 8cm (3 inches) tall, while I have not even sown mine. The banter that goes on between us is about how well our plants are growing, how many fruits they have and what the flavour will be like. I reckon that my 'Sungold' taste far better then his 'Alicante', and so on. We have a go at each other right the way through the season. It's all harmless fun really, but it does give us a laugh.

In the evening I went over to Writtle College to lecture to my RHS Advanced Certificate students about soils.

*

22 March

I was writing for a large part of the day. I wanted to try and get a number of articles completed, so that I felt I was on top of things. Then I am more motivated to try and stay ahead with my weekly contributions, and feel less pressured.

I never like being late with anything. I think this goes back to my upbringing. I was taught never to be late, as it is bad manners and puts other people out. Now, when I am having a go at a student for being late, I can often hear my dad's voice. I say practically the same words!

I felt tired in the afternoon, so I had a sleep. I set the alarm clock for 3 p.m., but woke at 6 with the clock still making its alarm sound! I suppose it's a long day. I am up at 6 a.m. and often do not get back into the house until 10.45 p.m., having not stopped all day. Then I still have to prepare for tomorrow. Luckily my over-sleeping didn't make me late for anything!

*

23 March

I took Tara over to Elaine and Phil's. They have always looked after her for me, and she considers their house her second home. They are both great animal lovers and they treat her as they do their own dog.

This is so nice, and it allows me not to worry

about her when I am away. I have always said that I would never put a dog that came from a rescue shelter back into a kennel. I do, however, realize that I am very fortunate to have the support of Elaine and Phil—and Reg and Louise—both of whom also sometimes look after Tara.

I then drove over to Northampton to see a couple of friends that I have known for many years. We first met on an Alpine Garden Society trip to look at plants in Czechoslovakia. Deirdre and Ed have a nice garden and we enjoy each other's company.

We had a pleasant evening meal together and the conversation moved on to the second series of *Christine's Garden*. Both of them had some useful suggestions, which I duly noted down.

Ed recalled one of his lingering memories of me, while on a trip to see orchids growing on a large scale, not too far from where they live. He says I was on the ground taking photographs and squealing with delight, kicking my legs in the air, and then jumping for joy and saying 'It's fantastic!' a million times. It sounds like me, I must admit!

People who have travelled with me know just how excited I can get. I have been known to stop a car, jump out, climb up about 20m (70 feet) in minutes and scream down to everyone, left wondering below, to come and see what I have spotted. It's only when I look down again that I realize why they haven't followed!

One of my greatest thrills is seeing plants in the wild. I am not sure why they give me so much pleasure. Plants can make me physically tingle.

In South Africa, on the Sani Pass, I went to photograph a gladiolus called *Gladiolus flanaganii*, whose common name is the suicide lily because it grows hortizontally out of cliff faces, and often falls off to its death. After I'd photographed this plant, growing on the cliff face, I was called 'Suicide Chris' for the rest of the trip.

The only time I really feel at peace is when I am out in the sticks looking for, and finding, plants to photograph. Many of my friends have often said that I glow with pleasure and contentment when out in the field. I just love wild places, the skies, the fields, the sense of freedom, fantastic plants growing in wild, sometimes inhospitable, places, the smells and the people with whom you communicate in a language of smiles, not words. This is really me. I love gardening back in the UK, but my heart and soul really belong out in the wilds.

*

24–26 March
Deirdre, Ed and I went off to look at snowdrops in several gardens around Northampton. The season is late this year, so flowering was variable.

All of the gardens we visited were plantsman's gardens, just dripping with really good plants. These are great meeting-points where people who are nutty about plants can get together and talk for hours about the plants they are looking at. I must admit that these gardens can be appreciated, on a very basic level, just for their layout and colour at this time of the year. But, the more you know about plants, the more you are going to get out of a visit to this type of garden, and the more you will appreciate the skill of the person designing the garden and growing these unusual plants.

We were seeing great varieties of snowdrops, hellebores, daphnes, irises, crocuses, spring-flowering shrubs such as camellias and some plants being grown for their stem effect. The weather was not too cold and the light was good for taking photographs.

In the evening I showed Deirdre, Ed and some friends of theirs the slides that I took in Iran last April. The friends were fascinated by my comments about the country's friendly people, great plants, lovely buildings and the large area of the countryside that is mountainous.

I enjoy sharing my slides with people as I relive the trip in my mind and remember the details. A private reminder of a tremendous trip.

*

27 March

I was in college all day with my Monday group. This was a theory day, where we covered information on ground cover planting, rock garden construction and water gardening.

In the evening I took Tara to the vet, as she had been sick. She has been very unsteady on her legs over the last few days and not eating, which is unusual. Now she is getting old, I worry so much about her when she is not well. Each time I take her to the vet I wonder if it is going to be that grim news that no pet-owner wants to hear.

After examining her the vet said said he thought it might be an ear infection and gave her some antibiotics. Once back at home, I took his advice and cooked her some chicken. She ate the whole lot!

*

28 March

I carried out two Horticultural Trades Association (HTA) Retail Plant Care Award Assessments today at a garden centre in Milton Keynes. One of the candidates passed, but the other did not. The internal moderator turned up to see me carry out the assessment. This is part of the HTA's quality control system to make certain that all assessors are working to the same standards, and are being fair in their methods.

During the assessments people kept coming up to me to comment on *Christine's Garden*. I found this to be a difficult situation, as I was not sure how the moderator would take these constant interruptions. At the end of the assessments he and I went to have a cup of tea to discuss the results and the methods I use.

I thought I would get in first, and apologized for the interruptions to the assessment. I said that I had felt uncomfortable about it, but was unsure what I could do without making the candidate feel he was in an examination situation instead of a practical assessment. The first thing the moderator said was that he thought I handled the interruptions really well, and that he, and the HTA, were very proud of what I was doing. I should just accept that people would want to congratulate me and thank me for the series. This made me feel so much better.

In the evening I was over at Writtle College with the Advanced Certificate students carrying out a practical on seed sowing under glass and pricking out.

29 March

Rupert and Jimmy came over for the day to chat with me about my diary and work I had coming up that could be included in the filming of *Christine's Garden*. Though they are filming me doing what I would normally do, they need to be aware of the various locations in the UK I will be working in, so that they can arrange travel details, hotels and what equipment they will need.

Rupert was very positive about the second series, and I was feeling much more at ease. I now understand the process involved in making a series, and I know I can trust Rupert to show me as I am. Rupert is still trying to find someone suitable as an assistant producer, and I commented that he should try and get someone as soon as possible, so that he doesn't end up killing himself!

*

30 March

Sue Dougan, from BBC Kent, came to my house to carry out an interview with me. She asked me how, and where, I started gardening and how I got into radio. The rest of the interview was based on my garden and what it had been like filming a TV series about my life and gardening career.

The interview went well, and Sue explained that it would now be edited and she would let me have a copy once it had been transmitted.

I spent the rest of the day answering e-mails and phone calls, and sorting through my China slides for possible inclusion in a book on Chinese gardens. I managed to select 50 that I thought might be suitable, labelled them and sent them off to the picture editor of the book.

31 March

I went over to Buckhurst Hill, Essex, to complete some practical gardening at some flats that I have been maintaining for a number of years. The borders needed weeding through, and I pruned several shrubs which were getting too large for their positions.

In the evening I wrote my two weekly magazine articles and arranged an interview with BBC breakfast television for Monday.

APRIL

1 April
The weather is still very cold, and the season is late. Normally by this time of the year I have sown most of my vegetable seeds, and a lot of the annual flower seedlings are, by now, pricked out and growing on the living-room table. During all of the 15 years I've had this garden on the Hertfordshire/Essex border, the earliest date for sowing has been 15 March, and the latest, this year, 10 April.

My foxglove seedlings, which I had sown in a seed tray last August at 40 plants to the tray have now got to the stage where they need moving out of the seed tray and planting out. These over-wintered at the base of a north wall, without any protection whatsoever.

> I always water the trays before removing seedlings as this means less damage to the roots when you come to divide up the individual plants. The roots slide out of the damp compost rather than being rasped out of dry compost.

I planted them into the flower-bed, spacing them about 30cm (1 foot) apart under the purple plum tree (*Prunus cerasifera* 'Pissardii'). I just love the colour combinations of the pinks and the whites of the foxgloves, which contrast so well with the wine-red foliage of the plum tree. I planted all 40 under

67

the plum and now look forward to their display during the summer.

The lawn is now growing apace, and I am mowing it with the mower blades set as high as I can get them—although I don't scalp the lawn.

The weeds are starting to make themselves obvious, so I spent some of the afternoon pulling out chickweed and cleavers.

I find that, if I can get on top of the weeds early on and do not allow them to seed at all, this reduces the weed seed numbers in the soil and makes life considerably easier in the long run.

In the evening I completed a planting scheme for a client who has an overgrown shrub bed that needs drastic pruning and replanting. The aim is to bring in more colour, both during the summer and the winter months. At the moment there are several very large laurustinus (*Viburnum tinus*) that are so big that they are taking over huge expanses of the border and falling over and coming forward into the front of the border, as well as several lilacs (*Syringa* species), a forsythia, several very old oregon grapes (*Mahonia aquifolium*) and a lovely, but old, *Osmanthus delavayi* which, when in flower, must be out of this world.

The border, at the moment, is very green for much of the year and the shrubs that are worth saving now need a lot of pruning. This will be rejuvenating pruning, so as to regenerate new, vigorous, flowering wood to produce more flowers and hence more colour.

I have included new shrubs with colourful

foliage in my plan—*Photinia* x *fraseri* 'Red Robin', *Elaeagnus* x *ebbingei* 'Gilt Edge' and *Elaeagnus* 'Quicksilver'; autumn colour in the way of *Nandina domestica* 'Richmond', *Amelanchier laevis* and *Euonymus alatus*; and for the winter and spring *Viburnum farreri*, *Daphne mezereum*, *Sarcococca confusa* and *Chimonanthus praecox* 'Grandiflorus'. The last four plants all produce great scent as well as flowers in the dullest winter months. For the summer I have gone for *Hebe* x *franciscana* 'Variegata', *Lathyrus latifolius* and *Abelia floribunda* and then underplanted the gaps with a range of herbaceous perennials (those plants which die down to the ground each year and then produce new growth from the rootstock each spring). This range of plants, together with those which I will retain, should create a lovely picture right through the year.

I love completing planting plans. It allows me to play with colour, texture, form and plant combinations. I think I enjoy it so much as I have very little room, now, in my own garden, but, given a fresh canvas for someone else, I can indulge my love of plants. There are a lot of factors that I still have to bear in mind: the soil type, the aspect and the space available to develop the planting plan; the client's wishes in the way of colour; how much money they have to spend; how much growing experience they have; how much time they will have to look after the plants, and during which season they will spend most time in their garden enjoying it. There are a lot of questions that you should ask the client before you start creating something for them which they, hopefully, will enjoy for many years.

*

2 April

Christine's Garden has brought all sorts of things to me, and one of the most pleasurable is receiving e-mails from old friends that I had lost touch with. Today, I went to see a friend with whom I used to work with at an experimental horticultural station at Luddington near Stratford-on-Avon, way back in 1978, when I was a sandwich student from the Lancashire College of Agriculture (now called Myerscough). He now works, and lives, at the Rothamsted Research Station at Harpenden. This is the oldest agricultural research institution in the world. Founded by John Bonnet Lawes, on his inherited estate, it was set up to investigate the impact of organic and inorganic fertilizers on crop yields.

Richard had not changed at all and we had a great time getting up to date with where we had both worked since last seeing each other, and learning about family news. Richard had a young golden retriever puppy called Ellie and I had brought Tara with me, so that the puppy could meet another dog. The plan was to take Ellie out for her first walk on a lead, with Tara showing her what to do. We did laugh to see Tara getting pestered by Ellie, and then Tara giving Ellie a bash with her paw. Tara, being the older dog, was going to put the puppy in her place. It was a delight seeing them play-fighting together. Tara is getting old, and to see her run and play with a puppy gave me so much pleasure.

*

3 April

I had a 5 a.m. start to what was going to be a very long and tiring day. I was going over to a local garden, which opens under the National Garden Scheme, to do a feature for BBC breakfast television. This was a live broadcast, in which I chatted to the garden owner about the influence of the hose-pipe ban, which was imposed on much of eastern England today. I must say, broadcasting at 6, 7 and 8 a.m. is not something that I had done before, but it turned out to be a nice piece, which all enjoyed.

The garden owner chatted to me in a very friendly manner, and I described methods of conserving water. I mentioned that all plants grown in containers should have a plant saucer under them so that any water, which drains straight through the pot, is retained. I showed how lining a clay pot with several sheets of damp newspaper would help retain moisture, as would lining the sides of a container with polythene to restrict the sideways movement of water and evaporation from the pot.

> *Putting a layer of fine grit on the pot's surface acts as a mulch, which reduces water loss, and mixing water-absorbing swell gel into the compost at planting time also helps to reduce the problems that a dry summer may bring.*

Then off to London, to complete a consultancy for a lady who wanted information on what plants she needed to make her garden look like *Christine's Garden*. The lady had seen the series and wanted her beds to be full of colour all the season through. One of the commonest mistakes I see, when visiting gardens, is that people have borders that are much too narrow. This results in a lack of balance and height distribution. As a general rule, any border should be twice the width of the tallest plant being grown. So, if you have a plant 1m (3 feet) high, the border should be at least 2m (6 feet) wide.

Having completed that job, I drove up to Lancashire to my family home. I was giving a lecture to my original horticultural society in Rishton. It was so strange seeing my junior school teachers sitting in front of me. They told me how proud they all felt about me, and I found this quite moving. People I only remembered as a child came and chatted to me after the talk, reminiscing about my allotment and how they bought vegetables, flowers and plants that I raised there. They recalled my activities at the local flower show, where I was the show secretary at 13 years old! Some mentioned the lectures I gave to local horticultural societies, the first one when I was 17. I used to turn up on a moped before I graduated to a motorbike.

I crawled into bed at about 1.30 a.m. feeling very tired; happy to have had such a fulfilling day, reliving some very happy memories and meeting teachers and friends whom I had not seen in years and years. What moved me most, however, was the immense sense of pride that they all expressed in me.

*

4–7 April

Having driven up north, I decided to spend the week visiting friends whom I had not seen in ages. I went to Garstang to see Ben Andrews, my former lecturer, who featured in the first series of *Christine's Garden*. Ben and his wife Sue showed me round their garden, which was very different from when I had last seen it during filming in August 2005. Several very good shrubs were in flower, such as *Stachyurus praecox* with its long yellow catkins showing their true glory. Their camellias were looking good, too, and the fresh growth on the many and varied trees and shrubs was a delight.

We chatted about old times at the Lancashire College of Horticulture, about fellow students with whom I had completed my course and plants which we both grew, and generally enjoyed ourselves.

The following day I went off to see a non-gardening friend, whom I took out for lunch, and we then drove around the tops of Haslinden. It's when I go back up north that I realize how very beautiful it all is. Vast open spaces of wonderful countryside, varying from moor to grassland, the lovely Lancashire coast, hills and mountains. Not many people realize how lovely Lancashire is. It still suffers from the memories of the industrial north of England with its cotton mills. Well, eat your heart out, for it's a great place, with some of Britain's best scenery—or am I biased?

The following morning was bright, and I left my parents' home to drive up to Richmond, in NorthYorkshire. I was visiting a former colleague, George Brown, who used to work in the book trade, and who was responsible for publishing my first book. I hadn't seen him since he moved to Richmond, and what a lovely home and garden he has made.

For someone who is not a gardener, he has used local materials very sensitively in his garden. He has used gravels and stone, planted in between with drought-resistant and low-maintenance plants. The combinations of greys and blues looked really good. He is not aware of it, but he was following two of the basic rules of garden design—keep it simple and use local materials—and, oh, how nice it is.

When *Christine's Garden* was being shown, I had an e-mail from a gardener in the north who had a clerodendrum which had not flowered. Knowing that this was a plant that did better in the south of the country, I suggested that the wood might not have received enough sunshine to ripen it over the past season, which was why it wasn't flowering. I also suggested that, during the growing season, she should feed it weekly with a potash-rich fertilizer, such as tomato food. Potash is the fertilizer which encourages flowering.

Well, what a surprise. I found out that the lady in question, Jennifer Capewell, lived three doors away from George. Round we went and I looked at the shrub and the rest of the garden. I ended up drinking malt whisky—another favourite pastime of mine—and then, while George went off to cook what turned out to be a great dinner for us all, Jennifer took me for a walk around Richmond. She point out landmarks such as the falls, chatted about the history of the town, the old town walls and the reconstruction of the bridge over the river, and then showed me the theatre.

Both Jennifer and George are volunteer guides around the theatre, and hence know the fascinating history associated with this building. The following morning George took me inside and we went backstage, where he showed me everything including the changing rooms, the lifting mechanisms for getting things on to the stage, the thunder box, the trapdoor and the movable scenery. We also inspected the auditorium and spent time in the little museum. Being shown around a place by a person who really knows it inside out, and loves what they are doing, brings the whole thing alive and makes it so much more interesting.

I left after lunch and drove back home, keeping to the old roads just so that I could enjoy the views.

*

8 April
During the morning I planted my potatoes. This time I have gone for the cultivar 'Charlotte'. I like trying cultivars which I haven't tried before. When you are giving gardening advice, it is so much easier if you have some experience of what you are talking about!

> *I always soak the tubers overnight in a solution of liquid fertilizer, so that they are full of water, and when planting them in a trench, I cover them with leafmould. This keep the tubers clean and also, I believe, helps retain more moisture around the roots.*

Some onions went in next. I always grow these from sets, as I cannot be bothered growing them

75

from seed. They are easier to grow this way, and the seed-bed preparation and growing techniques are simpler.

I then drove over to BBC Essex at Chelmsford to do a two-hour live phone-in. I do so enjoy live radio broadcasting. It's like chatting away to friends about their gardening problems, and I just love sharing my knowledge and being able to help people. I gain a tremendous amount of satisfaction from this work.

The questions were typical for the time of the year. Was it too late to prune roses? How should you prune a wisteria? When should you divide a peace lily? What type of compost should be used for lilies? How to rejuvenate a plum tree? What to do about very leggy sweet pea plants? How should you start off begonia tubers, and which way up should they be planted?

The questions that I always find funny are the ones from people who are trying to get you to identify something. Descriptions vary, and the professional's descriptions are very different from the inexperienced gardener's. I just love it when the person says, well, it's got leaves and they are green. That really helps! You then ask them what the flowers look like, and they say they do not know! In the end you just have to ask them to send you a bit. Once you have the plant material in your hand it is so much easier, except when the person sends you the sample wrapped in wet kitchen roll in a plastic bag. Even I cannot identify green soup!

During the New Year, when I was broadcasting at BBC Essex, I set a question for the weekly competition, the prize for which was for two couples to come into the studio to see how the programme was made, and then to come back home with me for afternoon tea and a look round my garden. The four people all brought me something as a 'thank-you'—freshly made cakes, home-produced eggs and a plant.

I do so love being given things which reflect the person giving them. I would rather have a pot of home-made jam than a box of sweets, or similar, bought from a shop. It is a giving of themselves.

In preparation for sowing tomorrow, I brought the compost indoors, into the kitchen, to warm it up.

*

9–10 April

I spent most of the morning sowing the remaining vegetable seeds outdoors—lettuce, radish, spring onions, leeks, peas, parsnips and carrots. These rows tend to be spaced only 30cm (1 foot) apart, as I do not need particularly large items of anything. Plant spacing influences size and quality enormously, so an understanding of the basic principles is important if you wish to manipulate the final size of the vegetable at harvest.

Indoors, on the dining-room table, the runner beans, courgettes, squash, pumpkins and tomatoes were sown into small individual pots or modules.

For sowing seeds I always use compost that has been sitting in the kitchen overnight so it is warm. I have found that if I use it straight out of the shed, where it is stored, it is very cold and

77

delays the start of growth by as much as
six days. I also water all the pots, etc.,
with lukewarm water for the same
reason.

In the afternoon I drove up to Clayton West near Huddersfield with Rupert and Jimmy to spend the evening at a local motel. Tomorrow would be our first day to start filming the second series of *Christine's Garden*.

When we went to check in at the motel I was greeted by the receptionist with 'Hello, Christine'. This rather took me aback. The lady said it was like greeting a friend, as she had watched all of *Christine's Garden* and felt she knew me personally. I was surprised by this, but felt rather touched. Rupert and Jimmy commented on the influence of TV on people's lives.

Once we had all settled in, we went for our evening meal. We talked about the filming, and Rupert and Jimmy chatted away about films and programmes they have seen and been involved with. This is another world to me, and I enjoy seeing the lads chatting away about their world with as much enthusiasm as I do about my world.

After the main course, the waitress came and took our dessert orders. I decided I would have cheese and biscuits. This turned out to be quite funny, as long as you had a sense of humour. When it arrived, we all nearly died. Cheese and biscuits was one of the most expensive items on the dessert menu and, when it came, the portion was tiny. I commented to the lads that it must have been really difficult to cut cheese so thin! When the waitress came back to ask whether everything was all right, Rupert commented on the cheese and biscuits, and said it would be nice to have more cheese. Off she went, and returned with just one more sliver. How we all contained ourselves I do not know. It was the most expensive three slivers of cheese I have ever eaten and, at the end of the day, it was only mousetrap! It was a shame, as I am sure we will be eating there again, but I will not be ordering the cheese.

*

11–12 April

What an amazing two days these were. We all drove from the motel up to the Kirklees Light Railway, at Clayton West, to meet the owners, and I discussed developing the horticultural interest of the site. The intention is also to engage the enthusiasm, skill and knowledge of the present volunteers and members of the local horticultural society, in developing this very beautiful strip of Yorkshire (yes, I did write Yorkshire) countryside (remember I am a Lancastrian!).

The present owners have had the site since January 2006, and have come to realize that they will need assistance with the management of the vegetation along the 13km (8 miles) or so of line. The areas around the main station, and other stopping places along the line, need developing, plus a few other habitats and areas.

The owners watched me during my first series, and apparently said to each other, 'If she can turn us on as non-gardeners, she's the lass to get involved with this project.' They made contact with me, numerous e-mails and phone calls followed, and this two-day visit is the result.

It could be extremely thrilling, but it is an enormous project, probably needing between five and ten years to pull off all my ideas. Having been up and down the line, travelling on the little trains (15-inch gauge), I would really like to develop it as a Yorkshire wild flower reserve, using only native wild flowers that grow, and have been recorded, in that location. The challenge will be to research, and then locate, wild flower seeds that have been collected from plants grown locally.

Much is written on provenance, but research is now showing that, if plants are not to become invasive, but are to grow well and cope with local ecological conditions, then they should be grown from seed collected in the region.

As a horticulturist, this is an extremely responsible role, and I feel very deeply that I should do my utmost to ensure we get this project right. I would like to think that, in 20 years' time, someone will say this site is really good and the designer knew what they were doing. Fancy being able to stand here, and say I influenced this! That would be the ultimate reward for the successful use of horticultural knowledge and experience.

What attracted me especially was the love and passion of all the volunteers who work here. They all have steam gushing from their pores! They love this site, and the steam engines and all that is involved, as much as I love plants. What a thrill it could be to be part of this project.

In the evening I gave a talk to about 100 possible volunteers and horticultural society members about my thoughts and feelings, and what I felt should happen to the site. I would like it to be their site. Somewhere they can have a sense of belonging;

somewhere they could bring their kids and grandchildren, and say, 'I planted that.'

I would love kids to be able to come to the site and see the same flowers growing as I did as a child in the countryside, to make daisy chains with their mums and dads on a summer's day.

I would like horticulturists and garden-lovers to want to come and see what can be achieved with wild native flowers. I want the people involved to grow the plants from seed themselves, so that they feel a sense of ownership and love the plants. In that way they will look after the site, in the long term, and feel they want to keep coming back.

I found these two days of filming fascinating, as I had been wondering if I would still be able speak to the camera and be natural again, having seen the first series, and seen what I looked like on television. When we started, it was strange—I felt that I had never been away from filming. I just fell right into it again.

I think this really reflects the high esteem I have for the people working, and filming, around me. They are great professionals who are constantly trying to produce the very best. Rupert, Jimmy and I know each other now, and know how we work together as a team. Rupert can get the best out of me in a relaxed manner. At the end of two days' filming, I felt tired but happy that I could do it for a second time!

Despite this, although we have learned a lot from each other, there are times when we still do

81

not understand each other's worlds, and do not see things with the same eyes. During the two days of filming, we had commented on the old apple trees which grow along the railway line, and Rupert had said he would like to film one of the trees. We went to a suitable spot and Rupert started filming.

After he had been at it for some time, and I had been wondering why he was filming a mountain ash tree with daffodils growing underneath it, I asked him why he was filming this tree. He said he wanted to film the apples as I had commented on them. I then looked at him and said, pointing to the apple tree, which was about 6m (20 feet) away, 'That's the apple tree!' He just looked at me, exasperated, threw his hands in the air and said I should have told him.

I replied that I thought he was trying to capture the spring colour with the daffodils, which did look nice growing under the mountain ash tree, before going on to film the apple tree! Rupert just hasn't got a clue about plants, often resulting in obvious comic blunders.

We both have so much to learn about each other, and our very different way of seeing things. I need to learn about television making, and he and the gang about gardening. It's a good job we all have a sense of humour and fun, and a high level of tolerance and patience.

*

13–15 April
Home again, and much of this time was spent putting together a report for the owners of the railway, doing research and reliving the place and people whom I had met. This is extremely

premature. The owners need the report to see if what I am suggesting is OK for them, before they formally ask me to be involved.

I do so hope they will. It's a fantastic opportunity to actually improve a bit of England and to work with such lovely people. The warmth, openness, encouragement and enthusiasm shown, by all the people I met during the two days, were great.

I just loved the stationmaster, and all the other guys dressed as they would have been when working at the station in bygone days. Peter, the stationmaster, wore a bowler. I hadn't seen a guy in a bowler for years. It all created a very nostalgic feeling of a glorious time past.

Ian, the chief engineer and operational manager, is such a lovely man. He eats, sleeps, dreams, breathes and exudes the little trains, the landscape and his colleagues. I just love people who have a passion for what they do.

There can be no greater gift in life than to be able to work at something which becomes a way of life rather than a job. Some of us, including myself, are extremely lucky.

*

16–17 April

A great time was spent visiting friends and seeing how their gardens are developing. First to Harrow to see two friends, Frances and her sister, Eleanor, whom I met last year on a trip I led to China. We looked at each other's photographs of the trip, ate a lot of good food and drank a lot of excellent wine. We also chatted about my life since we last saw each other, and I enjoyed being taken round the garden by Frances, who obviously loves her plants.

I gain so much pleasure out of seeing other people enjoying plants. They do not have to be fantastically rare, or special, plants, just plants that turn their owners on. Frances's garden is simple but laid out in a fashion which she can look after and enjoy. And what enjoyment she gets from it. Just chatting to her indicated how much her garden meant to her.

My next visit was to spend the afternoon and evening with two of my past students who are creating two acres of garden near Colchester, and what a super job they are making of it. I have been visiting them for about five years now, and the garden is taking shape, looking really good and is a great credit to them.

As we walked round the garden, we shared the sight of the beautiful daffodils they had planted in great drifts. Geoff knows my views on planting single colours together and when we walked into the daffodils he was surprised that I did not comment on the planting they had done.

The planting did not attract my criticism, as Julie and Geoff had kept the colours and cultivars separate to each other, and, although they only had a bit of space between them, in the setting where they were, they looked OK. Remember, both of these gardeners have spent four years attending my lectures and it is obvious that they took in most of what I told them. What pleases me is that they are thinking about what I told them, but are capable of making up their own minds about what works in their particular garden.

In one area snake's head fritillary has now

established and, to my surprise, lily beetles were copulating on these plants. This was very early in the year. Let's just say they had a short, but very happy, existence together! If left, they would have totally defoliated the bulbs and reduced their growth, and possibly survival, next year. The best way of dealing with them is hand picking and destroying them.

Other areas in the garden that were looking good include the camellias, the woodland and, outside their house, the great drift of primroses that have seeded themselves along the driveway. These were looking fantastic, and are one of the great pleasures of spring.

In the evening Julia cooked us a very good meal, after which we sat together and went on a fanciful journey to Iran, via the slides that I had taken during my three weeks spent there last April. It always gives me great pleasure to share my slides of journeys around the world, with people who are interested. It's no good going to these places and then not sharing what you have seen and learned.

The Iranians are such friendly people and were very pleased to see us. We were treated very well, made to feel welcome wherever we went and experienced nothing that would stop me from jumping on a plane to go out there at the first opportunity. The wild flowers are lovely, and the countryside, along with fantastic architecture, makes this a country that everyone should visit.

*

18 April

Most of today was spent writing magazine articles. I sometimes find that when I start to write, nothing seems to come. What I have learned, over many years, is to leave it, go off and do something else. Eventually, when I return to the computer, I find I can manage to write something OK.

I often try to produce several articles at a time. This makes it easier for me to keep on top of things. I am the sort of person who does a million and one things. If I can get on top of some aspects of my work, it takes the pressure off slightly.

Another feature of my work is that I have to prepare well ahead of time. Things like lectures and training material need to be prepared in advance, and plant identification requests for college, practical request forms etc. often have to be submitted a week or two ahead of the date on which the items are needed. I am constantly working ahead of myself, and have to plan things with considerable efficiency.

During the evening I went over to Writtle College to complete a practical class with my RHS Advanced Certificate students. I started the class by showing the students how to 'pot off'. This is where you move a seedling or cutting from the tray in which it was sown or rooted, into its first plant pot. The students need to be able to answer these questions: is the plant going into the correct size of pot? Is the compost the correct type? When potted, is the plant sitting in the centre of the pot, at the correct depth, and has it been watered correctly?

Next, I showed the students how to repot a plant. This involves moving a plant from one pot into another the next size up, once the first pot has become full of roots. Normally, when the roots start coming though the holes in the bottom of the pot it is growing in, a plant needs to be moved on into the next size up. This gives the plant's root system much more room to develop and grow, and provides a new source of nutrients to exploit.

These techniques were then practised by the students.

*

19 April

I had a fascinating morning carrying out a consultancy on a 16th-century property with a very large garden. The owner had contacted me partly because she wanted to find out why a lot of her plants were dying, and also because she needed some new ideas, and planting suggestions, for several areas around the house.

I love it when I get involved with this type of detective work. You never really know what you are going into, but you have to draw on all the knowledge and experience that you have gained over the years, in order to work out what the problem is and then deal with it.

Big shrubs such as viburnum, taxus and eleagnus were showing symptoms such as yellowing of the foliage, die-back on one or more shoots and early leaf drop, or else just looking very sad with insipid-coloured leaves.

I asked the normal questions about feeding, and the lady said that she had only used mushroom compost over the years. This normally contains a high percentage of calcium, as lime is used in the construction of the mushroom growing beds. With this knowledge, I decided to test the soil pH to see if there was a problem on that front. Several test results showed that the pH range of the soil at the site was not responsible for the problems I was seeing. I then checked for pests and diseases and again found nothing to give me concern. Then, after I started to dig several big holes in the beds in which the plants where growing, came the moment of truth. I soon began to smell rotten eggs, and the colour in the soil was a mixture of grey and red.

These colours, and the smell, indicate that the soil is very badly drained, and also that, over the winter period, the water table rises to only a few inches beneath the soil surface. While digging, I found several partly rotted roots and the smell was awful.

This is a big problem, as the cost of putting in a large-scale drainage system, let alone finding an outlet to drain the water away, is really beyond the lady's means. As a short-term solution, I have suggested that she plants shrubs that are more tolerant of water-logged conditions, and, in the case of plants that will not take these conditions, gives them some help by planting them on a mound to raise the root system above the problem.

In the evening I drove up to Thetford to give a talk to the Thetford Gardening and Allotment Club. What a lovely group of people— they made me so very welcome. I was helped in from the car with all my equipment, and helped to set up, then given a cup of tea and welcomed by the Mayor and Mayoress.

After the vote of thanks, at the end of the talk I was given a lovely bouquet of flowers, and then invited to have supper with everyone. This was lovely. The ladies of the society, and local church, had set to and made sandwiches, sausage rolls, flans and super cakes. Tea and coffee were served, and then we had a question and answer session before drawing the raffle and concluding the meeting.

Before I left, a lot of people came up to me—not, as I was expecting, to ask me further gardening questions, but to thank me for making *Christine's Garden*, and for making Friday evenings so nice for them. Several people commented that it reminded them of their early gardening days, while many others felt it was a programme made about a gardener for gardeners. I was most touched by this.

*

20 April

Rupert and the gang turned up to film during the day.

I started the day by doing some research into the local flora at the Kirklees Light Railway. I am trying to establish what plants grow, or should grow, in the valley, so that, once I start to re-introduce plants beside the railway line, they are in keeping with the local plant life.

I am not a great fan of computers, but, for this type of exercise, the facilities offered by a computer are fantastic, and time spent on the web often results in some interesting facts. A few years ago I completed a basic computer course by attending evening classes at the local school, but what I have found is that, just like gardening, you learn to use a computer best by using it, not by reading about it!

I had a break and, having some post to send, decided to take Tara with me to the pillar-box. On the way there, I noticed some large patches of lichen, which I commented on to Rupert, who then asked me to talk about what I had noticed on my walk so far.

I pointed out the so-called weeds in the pavements, and along the kerb side (weeds are only plants growing where you do not want them to be). There were dandelions (*Taraxacum officinale*), chickweed (*Stellaria media*), herb Robert (*Geranium robertianum*), red clover (*Trifolium pratense*) and shepherd's purse (*Capsella pastoris*), all growing very happily.

Rupert remarked that I always seem to notice plants, nearly everywhere I go. I replied that I, naturally, see things that are green. Plants will grow practically everywhere and, if you start looking around your environment, you will see them—in walls, in brickwork and paving stones, alongside the road, in gutters, growing on chimney pots, by stream sides—everywhere, if you just look.

I had a meeting with a theatrical agent who came to discuss the possibility of my doing some one-night stands in theatres around the UK. He was talking about 'An evening with Christine of *Christine's Garden*' or something like that. We discussed format and content, and he asked me if I would be prepared to give it a try. I agreed to, and then we looked at dates etc.

This new venture could be an interesting challenge. The first part of the evening would be spent talking about my life so far, and answering questions that people would like to ask me about myself. Then we would have a break, and the second half would be a question-and-answer session on gardening topics. I see this as an extension of what I do already, in some ways, when

I am lecturing to local Women's Institutes, gardening clubs, horticultural societies and so on.

In the evening I went over to college to lecture to my first-year students. We are steadily working our way through soils, pests and diseases.

*

21 April

I woke early, so I went out into the garden to see what was happening. I noticed the *Arum creticum* in flower. This plant has lovely yellow flowers, and is very exotic looking. I grow a number of the arum family and find the flower structure and colour variation fascinating.

My peas in the dining-room had germinated, and I moved them out into the cold frame so they could get used to growing at cooler temperatures. I also moved the cuttings of my half-hardy perennials outside. These included abutilons, begonias, fuchsias, geraniums, bidens and petunias.

Having noticed that the sweet peas were getting leggy, I pinched out the growing points so they would develop into nice bushy plants. Outside, by the front door, I have an *Escallonia* 'Iveyi'. The new growths were getting very long, so I cut all of these back by half. I train this shrub against a wall, as I do not want it to get too large.

My copy of *Garden News* dropped through the letterbox, and as it included an article in which I had commented on Reg's tomatoes, I went round to show it to him. Reg gets such a thrill when he sees that I have mentioned him in something that I have written. I do not think he really believes me when I nip round and ask him if I can take photographs of him or his plants. One of the great

91

pleasures I get out of working on *Christine's Garden*, and all that has come out of it, is the happiness that this gives to Reg. He just loves doing the filming and having his photograph taken! What is great is that he looks so good and comes across just as he is.

We had a look at his garden, and already, up in the vegetable patch, his broad beans, carrots, leeks and potatoes were appearing through the soil, and about 8cm (3 inches) high. I told Reg that he should earth up his potatoes to protect them from the frost.

You do this by pulling soil over the shoots to bury them. This protects them from the frost and also encourages the production of longer stems, and thus a better crop, because the longer the stem, the greater the yield.

Louise has decided to follow Reg's and my example and grow some vegetables, and has sown carrots and salad leaves. Unfortunately, she has also sown French beans, courgettes and ridge cucumbers outside in the garden. I say 'unfortunately', because at this time of the year these plants need to be sown under glass, in heat, or on the kitchen windowsill, as it is still too cold to sow them outdoors. And this year is a late season. I mentioned this to Louise, who replied that it said 'sow them' on the seed packet!

I explained that it also said on the packet that they are tender plants and they should be sown at a certain temperature, but she told me that, when Reg had said to sow them, she did not realize that he meant indoors.

Reg then decided we should have a glass of wine together. We all chatted about vegetable growing, and how long it takes to build up experience. I told Louise that you learn to garden by gardening, and not by reading about it, or even going to evening classes or college. It's like most things in life: you get better at it with practice.

Reg has told Louise that, once he is too old to cope with all the land he has, she can have some of it (as her garden adjoins his), so that she can grow her vegetables there. At the moment she is growing mainly flowers in her garden, with just a few vegetables, in raised beds, by the kitchen door.

22 April

I went into college for a practical day with my RHS Advanced Certificate students. We spent the entire day on outdoor seed-bed preparation and then seed sowing in drills, before preparing the ground for sowing an annual border.

I split the class into half, so that each group could sow a border using one of the two different methods that are practised. In one method, you sow the seeds in rows, and then move seedlings to fill the allotted space, while in the other method you broadcast the seed all over the space available.

I was keen to show the students just how difficult the second method can be, when you broadcast the seed randomly. The trouble is that, once your seedlings start to grow, so do the weed seedlings and, unless you are really good at identifying young seedlings, it is almost impossible to tell which plants you want to keep. When the seeds are sown in rows, the weeds are easier to distinguish from the seedlings you want, and can be removed.

23 April

Tara had not been very well over the past two days and she was staggering about. I could not decide if she had experienced a small stroke, or if there was something wrong with her ears, so I took her to the vet. I must say that, on the way there, I was not sure that I was going to be bringing her home, and I was very worried and upset.

I sat with her in the waiting-room, stroking her head, just hoping that she was not as bad as I feared. She hates going to the vet, and always trembles and pants. This upset me even more.

By the time I got into the surgery, I was nearly in tears, and I think the vet could tell I was upset, as he asked if I would like a cup of tea. At this, I thought he was going to say that he would have to put Tara to sleep. I burst into tears and he asked me what the matter was. I told him, and he said that he didn't think that this was the case. He examined her and confirmed that she had not had a stroke. Further examination showed that she had an inner ear infection. He gave her an injection, and some tablets, and I brought her home. She slept for the rest of the day.

Once I got home, I pricked out some of my bedding plants from the seed tray in which they had been sown, into a larger one, allowing them to have more room. I spaced them out so that there were 40 plants per tray.

In the evening I went round to see Louise to tell her about Tara. We had dinner together with her mother who was visiting. Reg and Pat then came round and we all chatted about the Coventry area, which is where Louise's family come from and, by coincidence, near where my mother comes from.

I then took Tara and Alfie, Louise's dog, out for a walk on my own. We didn't go very far, as I was concerned about Tara. I think the others had already been drinking wine before I turned up, which was why they did not fancy going for a walk with me!

*

24 April

This morning Tara was back at my bedside, pawing me to get up and let her out. I was delighted to see her so much better. She even ran down the lane on her walk. I was so happy.

> *Tara is old and I know what I'll have to face one day, but I hope she will go on a bit longer. She seems happy and wags her tail when we go out and loves being walked by Reg. She still enjoys her food. I will be so upset when that awful day arrives.*

Rupert and the gang turned up to film in the garden. Rupert was trying to catch the spring display. I did explain to him that he had already missed the snowdrops, crocuses, early scillas and a host of other early-flowering bulbs.

I think my garden is at its best on 5 April. There are so many bulbs out then—daffodils, crocuses, snowdrops, fritillaries, tulips, hyacinths, anemones, puschkinia, muscari and scillas.

Filming eats up film footage like it is going out

of fashion, and Rupert mainly concentrated on the garden and plants, and did not ask for much of a commentary from me.

While the gang were filming in the garden, I made various phone calls, organizing some hanging basket demonstrations, lectures and training and prepared a slide lecture for a talk I am giving in May, on 'Colour in the Garden'. I've been asked by the garden centre that is hosting the talk to let them have a list of the slides I will be showing, so they can ensure they have the plants in stock in case the audience wish to buy them.

I also had time to sow some seeds. I sowed godetia, calendula, pumpkins and cosmos. These were placed on my dining table. I do not have a greenhouse, so everything that I grow from seed normally starts off on the table in the living-room. I cover this with a sheet of heavy-duty plastic, and place all my seed trays inside gravel trays, so that the water does not run on to the table and the floor.

Also, I had time to nip round to Reg's to take a photograph of him with his tomatoes, so that I could illustrate an article I had just written about us all. I think there is going to be a bit of a tomato competition this year between Reg, Louise and me. Louse has only grown a few, from seeds that I gave her last year, but she is already talking about getting some more plants.

Reg's potatoes, carrots and leeks are all growing well. He always starts things off earlier than I do and, in the main, seems to get away with it. I tend to err on the side of caution, and watch the weather to see if frost is forecast.

*

25 April

Rupert turned up with the gang, to talk to me about what spring means to me.

I commented that it is all about the start of a new year, about the sight of new growth, and about the soil now being warm again to encourage growth and reproduction. It's also about having opportunities to try out new plants and ideas in the garden. It's about better light, longer days and freshness all around. It's about putting past mistakes behind you and, hopefully, having then learned from those mistakes, moving forward and trying again. I suppose it's about optimism.

I had some lovely *Fritillaria imperialis* in flower, and I told Rupert about the legend associated with this plant. The story goes that the crown imperial (which is its common name) was the only flower growing on the road along which Christ passed on his way to Calvary. The flower did not bow its head as Christ passed, and its punishment from then on was that its flower-head would hang down and weep for evermore.

If you look inside the flower you will see four beads of what appears to be water, hanging down from the top of the flower. These are supposed to be its tears! The reality of it is that they are its nectarines, secreting sugary water, to attract insects. But I think it's a nice story associated with the flower, and I enjoy sharing it with others.

I find it strange that a lot of people never even look

inside flowers, for in reality they are often missing the most beautiful part.

I then showed Rupert the lovely Judas tree (*Cercis siliquastrum*), which was in flower in my garden, and I told him another story about this plant, relating to its common name. Apparently, Judas was supposed to have hanged himself on this tree.

I also gave a piece to the camera about plant combinations, describing them in terms of an actor and a play. I pointed out that sometimes, after you've see a plant that you really like, and have bought it, taken it home and planted it in your own garden, it doesn't move you as it did the first time you saw it. I explained this by saying that what you had noticed the first time was the main actor being supported by other actors to the side, in front and behind. You tend to take down the name of the main actor, but ignore the supporting cast. With your plant, what you actually noticed was a combination of shapes, colours and textures. If you do not reproduce the whole combination in your own garden, the main actor is never going to shine.

I was teaching in the evening, and Rupert was still filming in the house and the garden at 5 p.m. I had asked him to finish by this time to allow me to get something to eat, relax a bit, walk Tara and get my mind around what I was going to lecture on. He was still in the garden, filming, when I left at 6.15 p.m.!

I have a tremendous respect for Rupert. He will not let go until he has got what he needs, and I admire him for not letting his standards slip—but at times I find him frustrating!

What I did learn from last year is that I must

speak to him about this. I know that, once I have explained the problem to him, he will do his best to leave on time. I have also learned, though, that if the light is right and the words are flowing from me, or if he has not yet got the very best out of the situation, or me, he will keep going whatever I say! I do admire this, as he is after the very best and the programme will be better for it.

Filming is a team thing, and the team players have to understand each other, and support each other. This includes making some compromises, to ensure that only the best possible result is produced.

✳

26 April

This was a very short day's filming. Rupert wanted to show me moving my tomato seedlings out of the pots I had sown them in, and into larger pots, in which they will grow until being planted out in June. They had all been sown into one pot and were now being moved to individual 8-cm (3-inch) pots, using multipurpose compost. Rupert also wanted to film me moving plants out of the dining-room into the cold frame outside, where they would get used to cooler conditions.

At lunch-time I went over to North End Farm, near Buntingford, for the official opening of their farm shop. I had been invited as I had previously given advice on business development and produce display.

I had seen Sheila on three earlier occasions, and it was nice to see her shop completed and open. She and her staff had put on an excellent lunch, serving only locally grown produce, including some of her own.

In the evening I drove down to Kent to a garden centre to give a demonstration on planting up containers and hanging baskets.

I had a horrendous journey. I was supposed to be there for 6.30 p.m., so that I could have a meal before the demonstration began at 7.30. As I was heading up towards the M11, the traffic was at a standstill. After some time, it became obvious that the motorway was closed, so I decided to make my way to Kent on 'A' roads instead. All went well until I got to the Dartford Tunnel. This too was partly shut! I phoned the garden centre to say I wouldn't be there till nearer 7.

I got off the M25 and hit road works. I tried the A2 and that was blocked. Eventually, several phone calls later, I got to the garden centre at 8.30 p.m. I got out of the car, was greeted by one of the most understanding owners I have ever met and went straight in and gave my demonstration.

The audience was very grateful that I had made such an effort to get there. I was unaware that local people had already been telling the garden centre that roads were congested, so I did not feel so bad after that. Once I had finished the demonstration, the owner invited me back to her house for something to eat. I was most grateful for this, as I had last eaten at lunch-time, and it was now 10.30 p.m.

*

27 April

I drove back down to Kent, to complete a garden consultancy. This lady had phoned me, some time ago, to say that she had a large garden but did not know which plants would grow where, and she was unsure about design. Could I help?

It was an interesting garden on a slope, with a mixture of borders and woodland. The soil was very chalky, and lacked organic matter, so it dried out very quickly.

For the borders, I suggested plants such as alliums, campanulas, irises, hellebores, iberis, lavaterias, pulsatillas, anemones, geraniums, rubeckias, thalitricums and verbascums. These would mix in well with what she had already and would extend the season of interest.

For a selection of shrubs, I recommended philadelphus, ribes, escallonia, arbutus, daphne, elaeagnus, weigela and lonicera.

I got home and walked Tara down by the river. I often do this after a journey; it helps me unwind and gives me a chance to think about my day.

*

28 April

I mowed the lawn, which seems to be growing well at the moment. It was a bit wet, as the morning dampness had not lifted when I started. I should really have waited another hour or so, as it would have been easier to cut, and the end result would have been better.

After cleaning down the mower, I then applied some parasitic eelworms to the soil, to control slugs and snails in the borders.

I am not over-keen on the use of slug pellets, so thought I would try these eelworms as a method of control.

Seed sowing was my next task—foxgloves, perennial sweet peas, poppies, variegated honesty and some campanulas. These are all hardy plants, and I put the pots out into the cold frame.

I went out to lunch with a friend I used to work with at a local garden centre. I worked in the advisory department, while Joy looked after the tree and shrub department.

We had a nice time catching up on each other's news. She is now self-employed, working as a gardener with clients between London and Bedford. She seems to be enjoying it, and has a good mix of assignments ranging from tiny gardens, where she only spends an hour a week, to estates that take her two or three days per month.

On getting home, I nipped in to see Reg. He was in his greenhouse. I noticed that side shoots on his tomatoes needed removing, so I had yet another chat to him about these, and showed him, again, how to do the job. I have great fun with Reg. It doesn't seem to matter how many times I show him how to do this job—he still doesn't get it right. I suppose it doesn't really matter, as his plants produce enough fruit for their own use.

The other job I noticed needed to be done, was to take the growing points out from his sweet pea plants. I mentioned this to Reg and we did the job together. This ensures that you end up with nice busy plants instead of thin, leggy ones.

*

29 April
I had a productive day. Because of the water shortage this year, and the hose-pipe ban in my area, I use my bath-water to water the garden. I

take the water downstairs in buckets, and this is hard work.

I keep meaning to get myself a pump, so I can take the water from the bathroom more easily than by my present method. Yes, I have tried siphoning it out, but I do not enjoy getting a mouthful of dirty bath-water, even if it is my own!

I then applied a long-lasting weed-killer to all my hard surfaces. The council does not always spray the kerb edge, so I also spray this. I am far too busy to spend time hand-weeding the cracks between my paving stones etc., so I spray once a year. I am careful with herbicides, however, and only use them where I feel it is necessary.

I drove over to Bedfordshire to see a friend for lunch. I met Gill when I first went freelance and she was my business adviser. We became friends, and I have since redesigned and planted her garden.

Gill's circumstances have changed over the years, and we have now replanted her borders through landscape fabric covered with bark. This greatly reduces the maintenance, and very few weeds grow. By using this method, Gill feels that she can still enjoy her garden without it being a burden to her.

In the evening I wrote my two weekly articles.

*

30 April
I spent a lot of the morning cataloguing and putting away six boxes of slides which I took at

Bodnant, Powis Castle, Wisley and Hyde Hall, as well as in my own garden, last autumn and this spring. I enjoy this job. It is good to be organized and it gives me the opportunity to relive, in my mind, the places I have visited and photographed.

MAY

1 May

I drove over to see my friend, Penny, who has just got herself a sheltie (Shetland sheepdog) puppy, called 'Indie'. She is a tricolour (black, white and brown) and she's very beautiful, cuddly and playful. I was keen to see her. Penny frequently visits me, and we sometimes go away together, so it is important that Indie will get on with Tara, but I couldn't take Tara over this time as Indie has not had all her injections yet. But I am most keen to see how Tara will cope this time with such a very small puppy.

I thought again about Tara's age and what I will have to face one day. I am wondering if I should get a puppy, too, to keep her company and, if I am honest, to make it easier for me on the dreadful day.

When I lost my previous dog, I felt so empty and devastated that I only lasted two days before I went and found a replacement, Tara. Having always had a dog since I was quite young, I do not think I could be without such a faithful friend and companion.

Dogs mean so much to me. Always there, welcoming me when I return home, sharing my walks in the countryside and giving me something to live and care for.

However, Tara may not cope with such a young

puppy, so I will have to chat to the vet. I'll also have to see how much time I have available. This filming lark for Series Two takes a lot of time. It might not be practical and I want to get a second opinion before I act.

*

2 May

I spent most of the day on my knees, hand-weeding a patio and pathway which is used as a feeding station for wildlife, including foxes. My client here is totally against using any weed-killers, despite my assurances that there are products which won't cause a problem to the environment. Today's task involved my using an old knife blade to remove weeds and moss from the cracks of the crazy paving. It's days like this when I recall people saying to me, 'Do you ever do any actual gardening these days?' I have the painful knees and back to prove it.

In the evening my students came in to college to complete practical work.

They were shown how to prick out seedlings. I mentioned the importance of using clean trays and sterilized compost to reduce the risk of disease infection. I pointed out the importance of the correct depth of tray so that the seedlings have enough room to develop a decent root system and utilize the maximum food source, without it being so deep that a lot of the compost is unused. Trays must be deep enough to ensure they do not dry out too quickly. The factors which dictate the spacing of seedlings are their size and shape, what plant it will become and how long it will stay in the tray.

I spent time showing the students how to grade

the seedlings to ensure uniformity in the tray. This is important in commercial growing, where all the plants need to be at the same stage of growth to receive treatment at the same time. The students then had fun trying to water the trays properly.

I will never forget my first day at a Saturday job when I was only 12, and being asked to water a greenhouse full of plants. After two hours, I went to find the foreman and said that I had done the job. The foreman asked if I had done it properly, and I said I thought I had. We then went back into the greenhouse and he said he did not wish to reprimand me, but there was a reason he had asked me to water that particular greenhouse by hand, which was that doing it properly should have taken me all day—so he'd know where I was! It did have over 1,000 plants in it.

We went round together and he picked up pots at intervals and knocked the plants out, just to show me that the water I had applied had only gone down about 2.5cm (1 inch) into the compost. He told me what I had done was fine, but now I should start at the beginning, go round again and then repeat the process once more. At intervals I was to knock out the pots to make sure they were properly watered.

I must say that it was probably one of the most important lessons in gardening that I have ever learned. Water is so vital to plants that not getting it right can really affect their growth, quality and yield. His comments left me with a skill which, over the years, has served me well.

*

3 May

This was a long day driving down to Kent to a garden centre to give two hanging basket and container planting demonstrations. Rupert and Jimmy came with me to film the proceedings.

I enjoy doing these demonstrations, as each one is different. I tend to go with the flow and say what comes to mind. I try to be funny and relate it to the plants that are available at the time, and to the level of knowledge of the people in front of me.

I am a traditionalist and I like the old-fashioned wire baskets; and I enjoy showing people how to get great results from them. I often ask my audience, 'How many plants should you put into a 30–45cm (12–18 inch) basket?' You get all sorts of figures, usually between ten and twenty. When I say anything up to 35, I can see people saying to themselves, 'She must be joking!'

I go on to show them that you put three to five plants in the bottom of the basket, another five to eight in the next layer, eight to ten in the top layer, one in the centre, then fill in the middle of the basket and perhaps add a few where there are spaces. You soon use up 35 plants!

For best results, I always soak the sphagnum moss overnight so it is saturated. That way the compost used to fill the basket will not be robbed of water when it's been fully planted and watered. The aim is to water the complete basket thoroughly, so that the plants establish well and the basket does not dry out quickly.

The type of compost I use is influenced by the type of plants I am growing, and how long the plants are going to remain in the basket or container. For annuals and bedding plants I tend to use either multipurpose or peat-free compost. For perennials I use a compost based on soil, such as John Innes No. 2, or, for shrubs in the container, No. 3.

I always incorporate a slow-release fertilizer in the compost, as I want a good display, and nutrients in the compost will soon run out if you do not add additional food. For fantastic displays I will also liquid feed at fortnightly intervals using a tomato fertilizer which encourages flower production.

Not only will I add fertilizer, but I am also a fan of using materials that will retain water. You can buy water-retaining swell gels, but, since I am a tight northerner, I take old sponges and put them through a mincing machine and mix this into the compost. Another trick I use is to line the container or basket with a sheet of polythene with a few drainage holes. This stops the water from evaporating out of the sides of the pots or basket so quickly. Using several layers of damp newspaper to line the inside of a container works well, too.

During the demonstrations, Rupert and Jimmy were filming when my personal microphone went dead—not the one that the public were hearing me from, but the one that was being used to record the sound-track for the programme. All of a sudden, Jimmy creeps in under the table and starts to fiddle in my pocket. What he did not realize was that the audience could see the top of his head! I joked with him and told him to put the fiver back in my pocket. The film tape then ran out, and Rupert had to stop me in full flow while he changed it for a new one. My audience were quite entertained and I think they were interested to see how a programme is actually put together and some of the production issues that are involved.

The three of us left the garden centre for what should have been an hour's journey back home. Eventually, after being directed off the motorway and spending hours stuck in traffic before making our way home along country lanes, we got back to my house at 8.30 p.m., tired and frustrated. Jimmy and Rupert still then had to get themselves home!

Filming is demanding and hard work. I often feel done in at the end of the day. I suppose a lot of it is because all the time I am thinking about what I am saying. We do not have prepared lines. Everything that's recorded is spontaneous, and Rupert is not always aware of what it is I am about to do or say. We film in a very free and natural manner. It must be frustrating for Rupert when he has, by chance, temporarily stopped filming and put his camera down, and at that very moment I say something that he would have liked to capture. Trying to get it a second time does not always work.

This style of filming, with its lack of predictability, and none of us knowing if I am going to give four minutes or twenty minutes of stuff, must be very hard for the team. They are so good with me and, I must say, they never complain or get annoyed. They are all very helpful and we have developed into a tight team in which we all contribute to the whole and are very supportive of each other.

*

4–5 May

Both days were spent filming in my garden.

Rupert wanted to film the garden as it was looking at that moment. He spent hours filming plants individually, and then took wide shots from different angles. What I learned from the first series is that he has the most marvellous eye for detail, and often sees things exactly as I do. I do not find many people seeing detail and colour, shape and texture in the way that I do. I feel deeply honoured that I have such a talented and skilled person willing to spend time with me, and record the detail of my life, in such a manner. Jimmy also contributes, throwing in a question that, so often, results in a good bit of footage.

What I also appreciate is that both men will share things of a technical nature with me. Jimmy will say something like 'You are off microphone', which did not mean a lot to me the first time I heard it. However he then let me put his headset on and demonstrated the effect that I cause if I move my head round too far when he is trying to record what I am saying. I find this fascinating and it gives me an insight into their skills and passions. It is so lovely to work with people who strive for perfection. I have a tremendous respect for them, not only as professional film crew but also the fact that both of them are nice, sensitive men who care about people.

Once Rupert had filmed the garden, he then asked me just to get on with what I had to do during the day. I started by repotting some of my rooted cuttings, which needed doing because they had started to produce roots out of the bottom of the pots in which they were growing. The plants

111

were geraniums, helichrysums, fuchsias, begonias and bidens. Putting them into a new pot gives the root system more room to grow and a new supply of fertilizer from the fresh compost.

When repotting it's important not to use a pot which is much bigger than the one from which you are moving the plant. So, if you had a 8-cm (3-inch) pot, ideally you would go one, or two, pot sizes up to an 11- or 13-cm (4- or 5-inch) pot. One reason for this is so that you don't want too much wet compost surrounding the old rootball. Another reason is economic—why give the plant more compost than the root system is going to use?

What a lot of people don't do is water the plant both before and after repotting. I always water my plants the day before repotting, and then water again, once they've been repotted, to settle the compost around the rootball.

We filmed in the vegetable garden, showing the newly emerging shoots of the broad beans, onions, lettuce, leeks and spring onions.

Indoors, my tomatoes on the dining-room table had started to grow towards the light. I turned the trays round to even out the growth and to try and keep the plants short and stocky rather than thin and leggy, which they can be when grown with insufficient light!

I then went round to see what Reg had been up to in his garden. His tomato plants were planted out into his greenhouse border soil and were about 30cm (1 foot) tall. All of his vegetables are much further on than mine, and he had been spending

112

much of the morning hoeing to keep the weeds down.

Back home, I went into the garden and found that my bay tree, grown in a pot, had started to produce suckers from the root system. These can sap the energy from the plant and weaken it. If left, they will sometimes grow more strongly than the main plant and can even take over. I removed the suckers by cutting them off with an old knife.

*

6 May

I was over at college showing my students how to prepare a vegetable plot for sowing seeds in V-shaped and also flat-bottomed drills. The students then went on to sow some lettuce, cabbage, peas and broad beans, so that they saw all the different methods that can be used.

During the afternoon, I asked them to sow an annual border. This involved preparing the plot, selecting the seed that they needed, planning for height, shape, colour, flowering season and drift size, and then deciding how many seeds to sow and which method to use.

Students often begin a task with apprehension, but I am always thrilled, over the day, to see them developing their skills and confidence. They produced a good level of work and had much to be proud of by the end of the day.

*

7 May

The bulbs are only just starting to die down in my garden, and I think it will probably be another three to four weeks before I can clear the beds and get my young plants, grown from cuttings, and the rest of the annuals I have grown from seed, out into their permanent planting positions. With this in mind, I repotted most of the plants at least one pot size up and some of the more vigorous growers, such as the bidens and petunias, two sizes up. This will mean that they do not get starved and will continue to produce lots of flowering shoots.

I spent a lot of the day pricking out seedlings such as wallflowers, asters, zinnias and dahlias and then potting on courgettes, squash and cucumbers. These have been placed in my little plastic greenhouse to continue the hardening off.

In the vegetable garden I have put in sticks to support the pea plants. If I do not do this, as soon as they are about 5cm (2 inches) tall, the birds come along and take the tops out of them. Using pea sticks keeps the birds off, and I usually get away without any damage. The pea sticks are old prunings which I have collected during trimming jobs over the winter and dried for use in the spring. I also hoed through the vegetable garden to remove the weeds.

My sweet peas have been ready to plant out for the past week and, at last, I have planted them against the fence in the vegetable garden. I am hoping that, when they are in flower, they will attract a lot of beneficial insects that will help to keep down pest numbers in the vegetable garden. I am not a great fan of using pesticide sprays and would much prefer Mother Nature to help me.

I then nipped round to see Reg and Pat and gave them some of my sweet pea plants, and had a cup of tea. Reg took me into the garden and showed me his carrots, spring onions, parsnips and potatoes, which are growing away well.

*

8 May

I have been in college all day with my RHS Level 2 students, preparing them for their examination. I spend a lot of time with them discussing examination technique, and how to cope on the day. I feel a great sense of responsibility towards them, and hope that I help them to feel more confident and make the examination day as easy as possible.

I feel that my job is not just to impart information but also to try and ensure, to the best of my ability, that the students know how to approach their exam preparation and also how to sit the exam. I hate thinking of any of them struggling and getting worried about their revision or the examination. I give them my contact details and with some I can spend hours on the phone, trying to put them right or just to build up their confidence.

> *I always hated exams, so I know what it feels like to be screwed up with worry and anxiety. I hope that, by this stage in the course, they can trust me and turn to me for help. When a student does this I always consider it a great compliment.*

During the evening I phoned various people to organize filming over the next two to three weeks and other work activities.

115

*

9 May

The early morning was spent pricking out calendulas, godetias, asters and some wallflowers. I water the trays the night before I intend to prick out the plants, to aid removal of the young seedlings. I generally space them out at 35 or 40 plants to a standard seed tray. This seems to be suitable for most things.

I moved rooted cuttings from the kitchen windowsills to harden off (acclimatize) outside. These included Petunia 'Pearly Queen' which I have over-wintered for the past two years out-of-doors successfully, although it is protected by the wall of the house. However, I also took these cuttings just in case the parent plants were killed by frost. What I have noticed this year is that seedlings are germinating in the cradle in which the old plant is growing, so I am going to grow these on and see what they do. Along with the petunias, I have put fuchsias, coleus, plectranthus and begonias outside to harden off.

In the evening I went over to Writtle College to complete a practical session with my RHS Advanced Certificate course. We planted out young plants, grown from seed, which the students need to see through to maturity, including marrows, African marigolds and sweet peas. The aim of the practical work is to provide the students with the opportunity to acquire practical skills and complete tasks using a wide range of tools. Each student has a plot to work on through the year and is responsible for the preparation, and subsequent cultivation, of all of the plants that will be grown on the site. The students had already sown the plants themselves and will now see these through to harvest, or until they are killed by frost.

*

10 May

I took a trip up north to visit the Rose Bridge High School in Wigan. This was at the request of the headmaster, Jack Pendlebury.

It was a result of the assistant headmaster Andy Hurst's grandmother watching the first series of *Christine's Garden.* She mentioned to her grandson that she thought I might be the sort of person who could help the school develop the horticultural side of things.

Andy spoke to Jack and then Jack made contact with me. What so impressed me about Jack was his passion to develop the children's skills. He was really interested in making sure all the children acquired some practical as well as academic knowledge. This is also important to me, as I did not like school and was only interested in being a gardener, not gaining paper qualifications.

He mentioned to me that, at parents' evenings, when on a number of occasions the children had their grandparents with them, it seemed they enjoyed gardening together.

At the back of the school is a grass field that has not been used for many years. Jack was looking at this one day and, all of a sudden, thought about the possibility of turning this area, along with some land at the side of it which is woodland, into a horticultural resource. This is when he made contact with me, along with other organizations including the old college where I trained, now called Myerscough College.

By the time I got to the site, 40 tonnes of topsoil had already been delivered, along with 50 railway sleepers, and some slightly raised beds had been made by some of the children. Vicky, the learning manager, had been with the children, and was being assisted by Bernard Pendleton, the advancement manager from Myerscough.

The topsoil had been moved by the children on to the raised beds, which had been levelled, and the children had already started planting peas and sweet corn. Myerscough had donated some vegetable plants, along with another local nursery. It was really exciting to see these young children working so hard planting.

When I spoke to them, I learned that some had already been gardening for three or four years and knew how to plant. This was so encouraging. Once they had done the planting, the children watered in the young plants.

The children mainly involved with the project will be from years seven to nine, which means 11 to 14 years old, and there will be about 100 of them altogether, which I find fantastic.

Jack walked me around the two-acre site, chatting about what he hoped to achieve with the resources available. I saw all the habitats there, including woodland and a large pond. The pond is partly overgrown by bullrushes, flag iris and aquatic weeds. I told Jack that it would be best if he got a natural water specialist to deal with this area, as it is a subject in which I don't feel sufficiently experienced.

I left the site at 7.30 p.m. and made my way to a local hotel for the night. I felt happy, stimulated and very excited at the thought of being able to work with up to 100 children and help develop their horticultural skills. I was really impressed with everyone I met. They are so interested in the children and want to pass on to them skills that will be useful not only in the workplace but also in life.

*

11 May

I met up with Jack Pendlebury, the headmaster, Vicky the learning manager and Bernard from Myerscough again, to continue our discussions on what they would like to see being developed on the site and to establish what facilities they want. I am very keen to ensure that this project meets their own particular needs.

At the end of our meeting, which was extremely positive, I felt that I had an understanding of the short-term, and long-term, aims. I will go away and draw up a master plan and I will try to set achievable objectives.

What is so exciting about this project is the care and interest shown by the staff at the school towards the children. I was also moved by the comments of one of the children, called Daniel, as I sat in a courtyard that was full of bluebells.

I was sitting there, drawing up a rough list of what was in this area, when Daniel who I had spoken to the night before came over and started chatting to me. As we sat on the bench some other older children came in and they started teasing Daniel for talking to me. One of the them said that he was a sissy doing gardening. Daniel replied by asking what skill the other boy had. The other child said he played rugby. Daniel informed him he didn't think much of that, and that gardening was a

119

real skill that he could use when he left school. I felt so very proud of him, but could not find the words to tell him. I have never before sat with a young lad—I am not sure how old he is but I suspect probably 10 or 11—talking about gardening as a skill. He believed in what he was doing and what he had learned to date. Oh, how I glowed!

I just wish I had found the words to express my feelings to Daniel. Perhaps another occasion will arise.

After lunch I drove back home, and had just half an hour in which to turn around and go off to Writtle College to spend three hours with my RHS Advanced Certificate students.

I got to college feeling tired, but went out on to their practical plots with the students to plant out the sweet peas, marigolds and courgettes that they have produced. The aim is to produce a cut flower crop from the sweet peas. The students planted them along single canes so that they can grow the crop as cordons to ensure they get the correct length of flowering stem. The African marigolds were planted out around the plots in an attempt to see some companion planting techniques. The students identified both male and female flowers on the courgettes and removed the males to encourage the production of more female fruit.

The students then moved indoors to note details of all the plants that needed to be recorded for their identification work. Each student must learn the following details to ensure they have enough information and knowledge when sitting their examinations: botanical name, common name, family details, the main diagnostic features of the flowers (colour, size, texture, when they flower), foliage (type, colour, texture and arrangement). Does the plant have berries/fruit? (if so: colour, size, season, use, is it poisonous?) Where does the plant come from? What are the plant's dimensions given five, ten, twenty years of growth? What soil type will it grow on? What position does it favour? Is the plant hardy? How can the plant be used? Where is it most suitable for? How do you propagate the plant?

*

12 May

This was a welcome day at home for me.

First, I planted my runner beans out. I always grow mine up wigwams, as I do not have that much space, and I find harvesting them from a wigwam fairly easy. Due to the dry weather I have added a spoonful of water-retaining gel to the planting hole along with a cone of slow-release fertilizer. I have done this in the past, when water has been short, and seemed to achieve very good results.

Next, I planted the squash and courgettes with enough room for them to be grown on the ground or to be trained up the wigwams.

My grass continues to grow at such a pace it is difficult to know where it is getting its energy. I probably mow it at least twice a week at the moment.

The next job was to plant up a number of summer-flowering containers. The compost had not been replaced in the two years, so I felt I should take the old plants out and replenish the compost, adding water-retaining gel and some slow-release fertilizer. 'Pearly Queen' is such a super plant, which makes as much as 1m x 1m (3 foot x 3 foot) of growth in a season, and can completely cover itself with flowers.

Into a large pot on the patio, I put the same compost mixture and I planted some *Fuchsia arborescens*, pink argyranthemum and purple petunias.

To try and encourage a lot more beneficial insects into the vegetable garden I have planted numerous sweet pea plants at the base of the fence which surrounds it. I have strung wires through the fence to support the plants once they start growing. I am hoping for an attractive foliage cover as well as a lot of flowers, which I can cut for the house.

13 May

I went to a garden centre in Norfolk, answering gardening questions all day. I really do enjoy helping people on an individual basis. The questions ranged from 'Why isn't my wisteria flowering?', 'What can I plant in a north-facing border?' and 'What's wrong with my amaryllis bulbs?' to weed control problems and even how to set up a site of special scientific interest.

It's always fascinating chatting to gardeners and sharing your knowledge and passion with them.

14 May

I went round to see Reg and Pat, as I had some old gardening magazines for Reg, and my first harvested radish of the season for Pat. Reg doesn't like radishes and he won't grow them, but I know

Pat likes them as much as I do, so I always take her some when I start harvesting them.

One of my favourite recipes with radishes is what I call a 'radish-nut-carrot mix-up'. I take several washed radishes and slice them, mix them with grated carrots, throw in a handful of sunflower and pumpkin seeds, a handful of mixed nuts and dress the whole lot with olive oil and balsamic vinegar. I serve this with cold meat or pork pies and lots of home-made chutney.

Reg had spent time during the week planting up containers on his patio with petunias, begonias, busy lizzies and lobelias. He had hoed though the vegetable patch, which I must say was looking remarkably good. We ended up having a pre-lunch glass of wine together.

Louise was also at home, so I popped round to call on her to see what she had done in her garden recently. She had planted some more tomato plants that she had bought, along with numerous courgettes. She had done a great job of planting the tomatoes, but then had planted courgettes every 15cm (6 inches) along the same row. When I asked her why she had done this, she said Reg had said it would be fine! Reg really makes me laugh at times. He has never grown courgettes before!

I went on to explain that the courgette will get to a very large size and not only would it completely cover the base of the tomato plants, it would also grow over the path. I advised her that there was nothing for it but to move the courgettes to another part of the garden where they will have more space.

Louise then invited me to join her and Colin (her partner) for a roast dinner. Being on my own, I do not cook a roast very often, so I enjoy just sitting on the patio with them eating nice food and enjoying a glass of wine and a chat.

Later I walked Tara down by the river noticing the yellow of the rape fields along the river. I hate this strident colour and think longingly about about the corn and wheat fields of my youth.

✳

15 May

I was in college all day with the Monday RHS Level 2 group. This is their final day with me before they take their examination.

I spent time with them on examination technique and answering their enquiries and worries. We then worked through various past papers and discussed what the examiners would be looking for. I discussed the meanings of key words, such as explain, describe, note, list and state, trying to ensure that the students read the exam question carefully and understand exactly what the question is asking.

At the end of the day I gave them my best wishes and my little talk about keeping in contact, however busy I may appear, and never hesitating to ask for my help. The group then presented me with a 'thank-you' gift—a bottle of very nice whisky—and said some very kind things about the course. What pleased me more than anything, was that they said they had not only all learned a lot but had enjoyed it as well. This is very important in my eyes. Yes, of course I want them to pass their exams, but I am especially happy when someone tells me they have *enjoyed* the learning experience.

Got back home, walked Tara down by the river and then potted up a lily collection that had been sent to me in the post.

I have not yet cleared the beds of the spring-flowering plants, so I decided to put the lilies into pots, with multipurpose compost. That way they can start growing and then be planted out in the border once I have settled on the overall planting plan.

I have decided that I will have a dark red, bronze, orange and mustard border in one of the beds and have already pricked out seed trays containing seedlings of *Dahlia* 'Bishops' Children', zinnias, dark red petunias, dark red verbena and potted up tubers of *Dahlia* 'Bishop of Llandaff'. The darker lilies in the collection that were delivered include *Lilium* 'Black Beauty'. This is a very good lily with dark, raspberry-coloured flowers. Each bulb can produce up to 30 flowers when mature, so it is well worth waiting for and planting early in the development of the bed, as it does take a little while to come into its own. Like most things in life, they get better with maturity.

*

16 May
It was a lovely morning, so Tara and I walked further than I normally do first thing in the morning. I was enjoying the birds and the fresh growth of spring showing all around me. Tara was walking well and her tail was up, so all seemed

125

right with the world.

My car then had to be driven to the local dealer and left for its yearly service.

When I came back home I pricked out some foxgloves and godetia seedlings and repotted a few of my houseplants that needed to be moved on into larger pots. Then I disciplined myself to attend to office work which had been accumulating.

After collecting my car from the garage, I drove over to college to carry out a practical session with my RHS Advanced Certificate students. They planted out tomatoes, which they had grown from seed. They have grown 'Alicante' and 'Gardener's Delight', both cordon types, which will require the students to remove the side shoots regularly as the plants grow.

Next I demonstrated methods of tree planting and staking, after which they planted a tree on their own while I checked their technique. We discussed watering and mulching as part of the practical.

Then we went into the greenhouse to prick out the remaining seedlings into multipurpose compost at a spacing of 35 plants per large seed tray. They were watered and then placed on the glasshouse bench, where they will stay for the next two weeks before being moved outside to the cold frames and hardened off.

17 May
A day spent doing all sorts of oddments, starting with the lawn. I still cannot believe the speed at which it is growing. Despite dry weather, the grass is very vigorous and a good dark green colour.

I potted up some geraniums and verbena into larger pots, as they were getting root-bound and I anticipate at least another two to three weeks before they will go out into the garden.

Next, I prepared for a lecture on 'Colour in the Garden' to be presented at a garden centre in Devon on Monday. I have tried to put together a talk that reflects the seasons of the year, along with some easy-to-grow plants, plus a few that will hopefully excite the more informed gardener in the audience.

On Sunday I am at a garden centre giving advice on all things about tomatoes as part of National Tomato Week. I am constantly amazed at the number of different cultivars there are nowadays. I must say that it makes giving advice on these plants difficult when you have no particular experience of some of the kinds that you are asked about. However, there is a limit to the number of tomatoes one person can grow and eat—even by my standards.

I am going down to Devon to spend some of the weekend with old friends Diane and Stuart. They are both gardeners and Diane has a lovely large garden with some very unusual plants. I enjoy chatting to her, as she is a very knowledgeable plantswoman. I love being able to photograph her plants and we normally end up visiting a garden in the area, so it's very important that I have the right photographic equipment with me, and I got it ready.

Then I spent time poring over maps thinking about which part of the world I would like to try and visit this year. I can spend days looking at maps and thinking about the flora. It can take me up to a month to decide where I fancy going. I look at books and study the range of plants (and the climate, as I do not enjoy trekking in the heat of the day). I discover when the plants I want to see will be at their best. Also important to me is the number of other visitors. I suppose I am rather antisocial, and prefer not to see too many people apart from the locals. I have several options in my mind at the moment but cannot make a decision.

I'm thinking of Ethiopia, Iran and Mongolia and each offer something different. Time will tell!

*

18 May

Drove into London with my assessor's hat on to carry out a 'Retail Shop Care Award' assessment on behalf of the Horticultural Trades Association. The candidate had been working in the industry for a little while, so had some experience.

These assessments, which take between two and three hours, are a practical test of the competence of the candidate, who also has to carry out a written examination. The two parts of the award are taken on separate days at the place of employment, and the candidate must pass both parts to achieve the award.

The practical test involves questions on such subjects as customer care, consumer law, retail security and health and safety. Use of fertilizers, pesticides, lawn-care and composts are all compulsory items which the candidate must get right. They then have to pick three subject specialities out of the following: garden tools and equipment, bulbs, seeds and baby-bedding (seedlings and small plug plants), houseplants, leisure goods (such as furniture, bags and other outdoor equipment), floristry, landscaping materials or water gardening.

This is a highly respected award that is difficult to achieve and requires a lot of time, effort and work on the candidate's part to be successful. Unfortunately the candidate on this occasion did not reach the required standard, and I had to fail him in this part of the test.

I find the most difficult part of my assessor's role is having to fail someone. I hate it. I am so aware of how it feels to fail, having failed several things myself in the past, and know how devastating it can be at the time. I try to let people know why they have failed, and also go through with them what they should have answered. Sometimes, they realize that they didn't have enough information to give the right answers; on other occasions they can be so upset that they do not really want you going over with them where they went wrong. I feel upset for the candidate, the employer, the HTA and sometimes myself when a candidate fails as I know how much time, effort and money they've put in. It's so easy and so nice when they get through!

I had a terrible journey back through London and it took me three hours to do 42 miles. Rupert and Jimmy were due to meet me at my home at 3 p.m., to chat over the progress of the series and to allow me to meet Sarah, the new assistant producer. She seems friendly and approachable which is good. By the time I got home, all three of them had gone round to Reg's and were having a cup of tea.

In the evening I went over to Writtle to lecture to my RHS first year students on fruit and vegetable production. I have an early start in the morning, so on the way there I took Tara over to Elaine and Phil, who look after her for me while I am away. They are rather like Tara's second mum and dad.

*

19 May
A weekend off! I went down to see my friends in Devon.

After a good journey down, Diane, Stuart and I walked round the garden and discussed the changes they had made. These had been influenced greatly by my past comments on a previous visit, and did involve some substantial alterations, such as the removal of several large trees, a number of large shrubs out of overgrown shrubberies and an extremely large, wide conifer at the top of the garden. The conifer had been replaced by a very nice summerhouse that fitted in well with its surroundings in scale and style and looked very attractive indeed.

*

20 May
I went for a walk down the lanes around their house and spotted some early purple orchids (*Orchis mascula*) in the hedgerows. This plant is always such a pleasure to find. There were a reasonably large number of them and they were complemented by lots of other wild flowers. I do so enjoy seeing flowers growing naturally alongside roads and in hedgerows.

In the evening we joined friends for their wedding anniversary celebrations.

✳

21 May

Met up with the film crew at Sanders Garden World which is near Bridgewater. The garden centre had invited me down to take part in their 'Tomato Weekend'.

Over the two days, people could come and see over 100 different types of tomatoes either as growing plants or as seed, and taste various dishes made from tomatoes. It was fascinating chatting to people all day about the problems and issues associated with the crop.

Several problems came up frequently: 'Why do the ends of the tomato fruit turn black?' This is down to a calcium deficiency brought on by irregular watering, and is frequently seen in plants growing in grow-bags or pots where it is difficult to ensure enough water is available without it becoming too wet. The answer is to try and even out the watering so that the plants do not dry out at any stage.

'Which variety do you like the best and why?' The answer's 'Sungold', a cherry type that is orange in colour. I like it because, in my opinion, it is one of the best tasting of the cherry types and, being small, they can be eaten whole, so all the tangy juice explodes in your mouth rather than on the plate!

'When should plants be sown if you have not got a greenhouse?' It depends on whether you have a bright windowsill. If you have, and can keep the plants warm, they can be sown any time from

131

March onwards. I find it is not the sowing date that is the problem, it's once the young plants have grown to about 15cm (6 inches) tall. If you have nowhere to put them to harden them off, this is where problems begin as the plants start getting leggy and thin.

Generally I sow my seeds between 5 April and 10 May, depending on the season and weather. I start to harden off by putting the plants outside for a bit during the day, once the frosts have finished, and then leave them outside longer each day until they are left out both day and night. If a cool spell or late frost is forecast I bring them indoors again.

The film crew watched me through the day answering questions, chatting to people, selecting plants for them and—the best bit—tasting various dips, sauces and relishes!

Once the garden centre closed we all drove down to a hotel in Barnstaple, to be within easy reach of another garden centre at Ashford, where tomorrow I am due to give my lecture on 'Colour in the Garden'.

*

22 May

At the Trelawney Garden Centre at Ashford I was giving the lecture and then taking part in a question-and-answer session. Again Rupert and team filmed me in action. Apparently I was very funny and even Rupert, who was doing the filming

132

at times, said he had a job keeping the camera still. I only wish I knew what I said—I could use it again! In fact I am a very spontaneous person, who never uses notes, so what I say is what comes into my mind, and that includes the humour!

*

23 May

We drove over to Woolacombe so that Rupert could get some shots of me driving along in the countryside. This turned out to be a much longer session than we ever intended as I kept stopping the car to get out and look at the wild flowers. This of course meant that Rupert was in and out of their car more often than I think he had intended.

I was delighted to see alexanders (*Smyrnium olusatrum*) growing along the coast road. The lime-green flowers are so attractive but are restricted to coastal regions. The Romans used the stem bases, like celery, in cooking. I then spotted thrift (*Armeria maritima*) on the cliffs above the road. I stopped and was all set to start clambering up the cliff face, but Rupert has more regard for the health and safety issues associated with working with the BBC than I do. So all I got was a frustrating glimpse, not a close-up encounter. Rupert did point out that it was not a safe place to stop, but that would not normally have been enough to put me off. I would have driven on a bit, found a safe spot to park and then walked back to climb the cliff. Perhaps it was the thought of climbing up there with his camera that put *him* off!

Driving on along the hedgerows, I suddenly stopped, having spotted something I had never seen in North Devon before—the three-cornered

133

leek (*Allium triquetrum*). I have seen this plant in large numbers down in Cornwall, but never in Devon. I only saw the one plant, at the base of a hedge, but there it was. I love seeing things in unexpected places, and I also enjoy seeing things that I have never seen before. It is one of the great pleasures of horticulture that, however long you live, you will only ever know such a tiny part of the magic that is out there. Some people would find this frustrating. To me the opportunity to learn something new all the time is a great stimulation.

We had arranged to go and see a lady who had been in contact with me following the first series. Gillian Adams is partially sighted and sent me a taped letter expressing her kind thoughts on the programme, and informing me that she was born at Writtle college where I am a part-time lecturer. Although partially sighted, she still loves to garden and I found this fascinating, so I decided to contact her. To cut a long story short, I invited her to my talk at the garden centre so we could meet, and the intention was that we would then go back and film her garden.

Best-laid plans and all that. Because I had spent so much time looking at wild flowers and the fact that we all had a four-hour drive back home, Rupert decided that it would be too much, so, after a very late lunch, he called it a day. I felt slightly uncomfortable with this, as I know the trouble people go to once you say you will be bringing a film crew along to see them. I didn't have a problem with his decision, as I believe he was right. But for the person who has been expecting a visit it is very disappointing—after all, the house has to be cleaned, the garden gone through and then all the excitement at the thought of being on the telly! I decided I would call on my own.

What a delightful experience this turned out to be. Gillian has a garden on a slope, so it is on different levels, and it has borders of mixed shrubs and herbaceous perennials, a greenhouse, a swimming pool and a lawn. For someone who is registered blind the garden was very well laid out and extremely well colour co-ordinated. Gillian recognizes things by touch and smell, as well as with the very limited sight she has. I have not had much contact with a blind person in a garden before, so this was an interesting experience for me.

Gillian had some pots of cannas, which had got too big and heavy for her to deal with, so I offered to divide them for her. When I had done this, Gillian gave me several bits to bring home with me. Now Gillian is among my many friends in the gardening world. We got on so well that I did not leave until 7 p.m., and this was only after Gillian's husband, David, had made me sandwiches for the trip home. People can be so kind and considerate. A good trip back, but I do have to admit that a four-hour drive after such an action-packed few days left me shattered. Got into bed at 1.30 a.m.

✻

24 May

In the morning I worked in the front garden, weeding and removing the old bulb foliage and wallflowers that had finished flowering. I then forked over the beds, applied some slow-release fertilizer and planted them all with African marigolds.

I am not a great fan of these plants, but thought it would be worth seeing how they get on in a hot, dry summer (which is forecast). The front garden is in parts shady, so I am hoping that the bright orange flowers may illuminate the darker spots.

Sometimes, I think, you have to try things before being certain that you do not really like a plant, so this is a chance for the humble African marigold to show me what it can do!

Having finished the front garden, I then went into the back garden and trimmed my standard ribes. This is a white flowering currant, grown on a 1m (3-foot) stem, somewhat like a lollipop. I trained it as a standard as I do not have that much room and, by growing it on one stem, I have space underneath to grow other things.

Trimming the ribes involves using a pair of secateurs to remove all the growth that is produced this year. I cut this new growth off to where I can see it growing from the old darker growth. This keeps the bush neat and tidy and stops it outgrowing its allotted space.

The rest of the day was making phone calls to the Kirklees Light Railway about the work we're doing next week. Their plans had changed somewhat from the last time I had spoken to them, so I also needed to tell Rupert about their ideas and the logistics of what was being suggested. It was now a case of using plant material that had been raised from seeds collected in Yorkshire, so as to keep everything local. After some time using the Internet, I found a source of such plants and phoned them to organize what I would need.

In the evening I went over to Elaine and Phil's to collect Tara and have supper with them both. We often do this and enjoy a bottle of wine together.

*

25 May

We spent the day at Louise's, filming the two of us chatting about her garden, her tomatoes and the courgettes that were too close together. We also filmed my comment that she had put too many slug pellets around her plants to be effective.

I used to work for one of the major suppliers of slug pellets, as an advisory department manager, so I learned a lot about this pesticide. The one thing that stays with me is that amateur gardeners constantly over-use it, scattering the pellets so thickly that the ground is almost blue. The correct application rate is one pellet every 8–10cm (3–4 inches), but very few people read the instructions. Used sparingly, they are very effective, and this also reduces the risk to animals or birds.

26 May

Filming today was in my garden. It was raining when the crew arrived, so Rupert went about trying to film the rain. Apparently this is very difficult. To be seen on film it needs to be coming down like it is going out of fashion. We then just filmed me talking about my garden and what was happening at this time. I seldom work in my garden in the rain, due to the damage that you can do when walking over soil when it's wet. You can destroy any crumb structure, and good properties, very quickly, because walking over wet soil squeezes the air out and compacts it together. It has taken me years, with the addition of a lot organic matter, to get my soil into its present good state. It would take me seconds to destroy all that hard work by walking on it when wet.

As it was raining, I moved upstairs to my office, and started working on both the Kirklees Light Railway project and the Rose Bridge High School project. Rupert, once again, came up with the crew and filmed what I was doing.

Once it had stopped raining, I took Tara down to the river on my favourite walk. Rupert filmed me and asked me to comment on what I was seeing and feeling on this regular walk. I mentioned the change in colour of the hawthorn flowers once they had been pollinated, turning from white to a pale pink. I noticed the rippling grasses on the distant horizon and the different colours of the vegetation. I described them as looking as if an artist had taken a palette knife and used the flat edge to spread the colour over the landscape.

*

27 May

A very rewarding day spent in Basildon, planting up a Mediterranean drought-resistant garden, with disabled access and seating, and with fantastic views across a lake. I worked alongside children and adults who had never planted anything in their lives before. I was there to help instruct all those involved how to plant. This was a project involving the children of the Northland Park Youth Council and Bella D'Arcy, a past student of mine, who is now working as a garden designer. She is associated with all sorts of community gardening

138

projects, getting children to plan, design and plant the gardens themselves. I am very proud of her.

Within the hour we had about 28 children and I have no idea how many adults, all working and planting away. By the time it was finished it looked great and was a real credit to all involved.

What was so rewarding about the planting was hearing children saying things like 'I thought gardening was boring, but it's fun and easier than I was expecting', 'I like doing this, it's good' and lastly 'Look what we have done'. I left the site hoping that these comments reflected the experiences of all the children. If this is a way to show children how to garden, and what rewarding fun it can be, then here's to more community projects.

Returned home and watched the Chelsea Flower Show on TV. This was the first bit of the coverage I had managed to see all week, as I had just been too busy.

28 May

I got up early and weeded through my vegetable garden before a friend came over for the day. Penny had brought her new puppy, Indie, to meet Tara and to see how they would get on together. Tara was very good with Indie, and did not seem to mind this little energetic bundle of fluff running about in her home and garden.

Penny and I then cut all the hedges in the back garden. I have a mechanical hedge trimmer, which makes the job much easier. Once we had completed the cutting, and had put all the clippings on the compost heap, we took both dogs for a walk down to the river.

*

29 May

Went to Southminster in Nottinghamshire at the invitation of a lady called Pearl, to see her garden and give some advice on it. The garden was full of very attractive trees and shrubs and was being managed solely by Pearl. Over the years she had arranged it so that, now she is older and cannot do as much, the garden is easier for her to look after.

After we'd looked at her garden she took me round to her friends', Mike and Barbara, to look at theirs. It was very different from Pearl's, having mixed borders full of flowers, a pond, a vegetable garden and, out at the back, a large meadow full of glorious wild flowers, including betony, wild clary, campion, stitchwort, dandelions, lady's bedstraw, hawkweed, willowherbs and yellow rattle. What a lovely sight!

We had lunch altogether, and then I was taken off in Mike's car to look at local garden centres. What an interesting experience this was. We went to little ones and to very large ones. What did strike me was the huge difference in price between these garden centres and the ones in my home area, which are very expensive in comparison.

As I was leaving, Mike presented me with a lovely acer that I had been admiring in one of the garden centres. This was a kind gesture and touched me very much. Yet another 'friend' joins the many, already present, in my garden. One of the nice things about being given plants is that they prompt memories of people or experiences associated with them. My garden is a constant

140

memory-jogger!

From Southminster I decided to drive up to Wakefield as, in the morning, I was due back at the Kirklees Light Railway.

∗

30 May

I spent the early part of the morning looking around the site of the railway and taking photographs. I use these when trying to visualize things. If you have a photograph you have a record of what is actually there, rather than what you think may be there.

I then spent some time with the general manager, Graham Hurd, discussing what he wanted me to do over the next two days, and what needed doing over the next few months.

By lunch-time, the film crew had arrived and we discussed what Rupert would like to record me doing. I asked Graham if I could walk the entire length of the line to see what wild flowers, trees and shrubs grew there. I had had a look previously, way back in April, but things had grown a lot by now and it was looking very different. The other reason for walking the line was to enable me to carry out pH tests at various intervals.

I needed to know what is growing along the line and the degree of acidity/alkalinity of the soil, to ensure that any plants I introduce will grow and flourish there. pH testing not only shows you if you have a limey or acid soil but also gives an indication of what plant foods are available.

I am constantly amazed that many gardeners don't carry out this simple test, as it is fundamental to getting the most out of the soil, choosing suitable plants and identifying any fertilizer requirements. You can buy a small simple test kit from any garden centre. The test only takes a few minutes and you can see the results and, by reading the information on the pack, take the necessary course of action.

31 May

A very busy day for me and the film crew. Graham and I decided that it would be nice to plant up the area by the turntable with wild flowers this summer. This is at the end of the line, where the little train is turned round.

I thought more about how important it is to me that I re-introduce flowers that are from Yorkshire-grown seeds, or plants raised from seeds collected from Yorkshire. I am very aware that, from an ecological point of view, this area of line can be very special if it retains a real sense of the Yorkshire countryside. However, it would be very easy to destroy all of this by introducing plants or seeds from elsewhere.

With the help of a volunteer at the railway—Maureen Dyson—I have carried out a lot of research into the local flora of the site, and am keen to build on this and not introduce plants that would not normally grow in the area.

With this information at hand, and knowing that Graham had invited children from two local schools to come along this afternoon to do some work, I set off over to Mires Beck Nursery at North Cave, who specialize in wild flowers and plants of Yorkshire provenance (those originating in Yorkshire), to buy some plants.

While at the nursery, I obtained some small

plants for the children from the school to repot into larger pots, take home and bring back at a later date once they have grown on. I would then like the children to plant those plants that they have grown themselves. It would be great if some of them were interested enough to come back from time to time to see how their plants were growing. My dream is that one day some of them may take their own children to see the flowers they planted, and may even get their grandchildren interested.

Back at the railway, I was greeted by lots and lots of children, teachers, parents and grandparents. Some compost and pots had been delivered. All I had to do now was bring some order, distribute the compost, pots and plants and show everyone what to do.

This was great fun. The children surrounded me, as I spoke to them. It was good seeing them all really listening to me. They were keen to answer my questions and I was very impressed by them. They all watched carefully as I showed them what to do, and then they went off and did an excellent job.

Once the potting was completed, I got them all together again to tell them how to look after the plants. I asked them to take ten plants each home with them. Some of the children came and thanked me, while others said that they had enjoyed the day. That was all I needed to make the hard work of the past two days very worthwhile.

Having cleaned up the site, I then spoke to Graham about the other plants that I had brought back. These included the giant bellflower, foxgloves, bugle, kidney vetch, water avens, ox-eye daisy, yarrow, cowslips, selfheal, salad burnet, thyme, germander speedwell and tufted vetch. In all, I selected 1,400 plants for this project.

Needless to say, when I finally got home and into bed, I did not take too much rocking!

JUNE

1 June

I worked for a client who needed an overgrown shrubbery cut back. This meant removing very tall shoots to ground level on laurel, *Kerria japonica*, dogwood, forsythia and flowering currant, removing brambles by forking out, and then shaping the border so that it looked attractive. Having removed a lot of growth, I spent the rest of the day at the grinding machine, reducing the material, and stacking it in a spare compost bin.

This garden uses a lot of compost, so grinding up anything that can be composted has reduced the need to buy in so much. We have estimated that, in one season alone, we recouped the cost of a fairly expensive grinder.

The other advantage of grinding on site is that it reduces the fuel costs involved in taking the material to the local waste disposal site.

✳

2 June

I spent the morning with the film crew, who wanted to see the young tomato plants being planted out into the garden. It was the first time, since starting filming the second series, that I wished they were not turning up. I awoke feeling done in and very irritable, having not slept well, and could have done without them appearing on my doorstep at 8.30 a.m.

When they did arrive, they asked me how I was, so I told them. It was at this stage that Rupert and Sarah said they were also very tired, and Jimmy agreed. We had been working flat out, recently, with heavy days filming and then often four hours or more in the car to get home! Rupert said that we would take it slowly and try to be more relaxed in future.

With only myself to feed, I usually only grow about eight tomato plants. These are placed in a warm, sunny spot out in the vegetable garden. I normally grow the variety 'Sungold', as I like the orange colour and the superb flavour. Planting, in a normal season, is completed by the second week of May, but the weather has been so cold this year that plant growth has been very slow.

I plant the tomato plants by taking out a large hole and putting the plants in quite deeply, with the first leaves (the cotyledons) just below the soil surface. This allows the stem to root and gives good anchorage. I place a teaspoonful of water-absorbing gel in the bottom of the hole and also a teaspoonful of slow-release fertilizer granules. I then return the soil, leaving a depression around the stem so that, when I water, the water does not just run off the surface (my vegetable garden is on a slope).

Each plant is staked individually with a 2-m (6-foot) cane pushed into the ground about 50cm (20 inches). I then tie each plant to the cane using twine or, sometimes, a sweet pea ring.

Rupert was having problems filming, as the distance between my rows is narrow and he has big feet! When I was seed sowing, I forgot about the practicalities of having a film camera placed in between the rows. I had to smile when Rupert was carefully watching where he was putting his feet, and the camera. Once, during the first series, he stood on a pumpkin, and I got really angry and told him, the rest of the crew and the BBC that they could get lost if they were going to stand on my plants and damage them!

Now, as we try to work with each other, we are often reminded of that morning. However, I still did not take them into account when I sowed the vegetable garden this year. I think the main problem is that, because it is my own garden, I just attend to it the way I always have. I could have made life slightly easier for Rupert, and the crew, if I had remembered the practicalities of filming and spaced things differently.

At lunchtime I went to see a student of mine and her small but well-planted garden. Sue has a rabbit, which she allows to run freely in the garden, so has found out that the family pet is excellent at pruning, but has never read a pruning book in its life! Sue deals with the problem by covering young plants with wire netting or, with larger plants, wrapping the netting around the base of the tree or shrub. I must admit that the rabbit is a lovely soft thing, but it wouldn't last long in my garden! I am not sure I could be as tolerant as Sue.

We then went round to her sister Chris's home to see her garden. I find it interesting that people talk down their gardens when I visit, or say they have spent ages getting them tidy. I know they do this as they think I am going to be critical. I seldom am, as each garden is very personal. I fully understand what is considered right and wrong, but in your own space you should be able to do your own thing. I felt that Chris had made excellent use of a small area by placing decking on one side and a big raised fish pond, surrounded by shrubs, on the other. The area felt right and provides Chris with a sitting area to relax in without being too much work.

*

3 June

I returned to Basildon, to Northlands Park, to carry out the opening of the garden which was planted last Saturday. What a great thrill we adults had when a lot of the children who had done the planting turned up to see their garden being opened.

The young people were praised by a local councillor. I told them that they should feel a sense of pride in what they had achieved; it was their garden and they had designed and planted it. I hoped that every time they walked past they would feel that they had made a valuable contribution to the park and their local community. I then cut the ribbon and declared the garden open.

In the early evening Louise and Colin called to invite me to a barbecue. I popped round with a bottle of wine and then Reg and Pat joined us. We all sat on the patio on the first really warm evening of the year. Louise and Colin had just returned from a week's holiday in Devon. They told me all about the gardens they had visited, and Louise showed me the plants she had brought back.

*

4 June

I was at home all day in the garden. Oh, what bliss!

I began to remove all the old bulb foliage that had started to die back. Research at the Royal Horticultural Society's garden at Wisley, some years ago, showed that, providing you leave the bulb's foliage for at least six weeks after the flowers have finished, the leaves can then be cut down to ground level without any deterioration. I have been doing this for years now and I always have a good display of bulbs each year.

I also removed the spring bedding plants, such as the forget-me-nots, weeded and tidied up. Once I had cleaned through the beds and removed all the rubbish, I planted out my summer bedding plants. I used the same technique I used for the tomatoes, adding a teaspoonful of both water-retaining gel and slow-release fertilizer to the planting hole. In this border, I have used a combination of plants including *Fuchsia* 'Tahlia', *Abutilon striatum thompsonii* and, mixed, dark red and purple petunias.

All the rubbish that I removed is composted, except for the roots of the ground elder that tends to creep in under the fence from both next-door gardens. This is a highly invasive weed that can be very difficult to control, when growing in between other plants, so I find it better to dig it out rather than trying to use a weed-killer.

After planting the summer bedding plants I watered them in well, and then collected all the empty pots and seed trays and washed them. I find washing them on a regular basis is much easier than leaving then until I have hundreds to wash, which I hate.

I am keen on clean pots, as it does

reduce the amount of possible
contamination from soil-born diseases.

∗

5–6 June

I went for a long walk with Tara down by the river.
I was out for three hours enjoying the sounds of
cuckoos, watching other birds along the river and
just looking at the landscape.

I stripped the middle bed in preparation for
planting it up. I have decided on a red, copper,
apricot, yellow and bronze theme for this area. I
have grown *Dahlia* 'Bishop of Llandaff', from
tubers. This is a deep red dahlia with dark bronze
foliage. *Dahlia* 'Bishops' Children' I grew from
seed. This is a mixture of fiery colours with rich,
dark bronze foliage. To complement the foliage
colour, I have put in yellow *Bidens* 'Golden Eye',
the flower colour contrasting with, and the ferny
leaves looking good against, the bolder foliage of
the dahlias. The bronze and apricots will come
from numerous calendulas. To give some height, at
the back of the borders, I have used *Fuchsia*
'Thalia' and, planted against it, for contrast, silver
Plectranthus argentatus. To add a bit of boldness,
and also height, I have added five *Ricinus
communis* 'Carmencita', one of the caster oil
plants. I am hopeful that the big deep brown leaves
and bright red flowers will look good amongst
everything else.

Slugs and snails are a real problem in my garden,
so I have treated the whole bed with a biological
slug-killer—nematodes. This you obtain by post as
a powder, which is mixed with water and applied
over the plants. I find that, once the soil is warm

enough, you obtain excellent control for about six weeks. If you apply the nematodes too early, when the soil is either too cold or too dry, it does not work.

In the evening I went off to teach my students at college. The RHS Advanced Certificate students spent the evening working on their plots. They tied in the sweet peas, thinned the lettuce they had sown previously, weeded and then spent the rest of the time transplanting seedlings from their annual borders.

To demonstrate the different methods of sowing an annual border, I had asked one group to sow their seeds in rows, called drills, and the other group to scatter the seeds over the beds and rake them in, in a broadcast fashion. The subsequent management can either be a nightmare, or relatively simple. The students who scattered their seeds had a very difficult job trying to identify the seedlings from the weeds. Believe me, this can take a lot of doing if you do not have much experience. These students must have been calling me things under their breath!

*

7 June

I spent the day with the news editor and magazine photographer of *Amateur Gardening*, who worked with me and Reg in our gardens. We then went over to Hyde Hall, near Chelmsford, to take photographs to illustrate the next three months' articles. The shots they take always seem to fit the articles I write amazingly well, and somehow it all fits together.

8 June

I stripped and planted up the long border, having decided on a pink, white and blue theme, planting a mixture of geraniums, busy lizzies and cornflowers.

Having used swell gel in all the other borders, I have decided to do the same in this one, but with a slight modification. Now that all the other borders are well watered I have noticed that, with the swell gel directly under a plant, as it has taken on water it has swollen and lifted the plant out of the ground. I have had to replant the whole lot, mixing the swollen gel into the soil surrounding the plants rather than beneath them. This works much better; I have not seen any plants pushed out of the ground since so this is the method I have adopted in the long border.

I keep coming back to that old saying, 'It's practical experience that really matters.' It's one thing reading about it, another doing it!

My large rhododendron 'Happy' has finished flowering, so I dead-headed it. This involves removing the spent flower buds to where you can see the new growth buds developing, normally just behind the old dying flowers. I use my thumb and fingers and snap off the old flower, leaving the buds to grow and develop. If the flowers are left on, these will develop into seedpods, which will weaken the growth for next year. Though it's a bit tiresome, and takes me nearly two hours, every time I see it in flower in the spring I feel it was a worthwhile

152

job.

In the evening I drove over to Writtle College to lecture to my RHS Level 2 students on garden design and planning. We looked at all the things you should take into account before undertaking a design.

These include: site analysis, site measurements, levels, aspect, climate, latitude, altitude, distance from the sea, rates of rainfall, soil, pH, texture, structure and drainage, views, enclosure, access, services such as electricity, gas, etc., client/owner requirements, available resources, size of the garden, maintenance required, aesthetic, recreational and utilitarian functions, conservation and preservation orders, historic features and present vegetation (what is worth saving and what is not).

This list started to show my students that a lot of knowledge and thought has to go into the project. They will receive two more of these three-hour lectures before we move on to the wider topics of use of plants and hard landscaping materials, such as stone, gravel, fences, etc.

9 June

I spent the day in the office. The weather was beginning to get warm again and it really was too hot for me outside. I like it between 21° and 24°C (70–75°F). By 11 a.m. I was wilting, so I retreated indoors.

I worked on the Kirklees Light Railway project, completed some work for the Rose Bridge High School project and wrote two magazine articles.

In the early evening I watered all my containers.

153

This is still taking ages because of the hose-pipe ban and, although I pump the water out of the bath and use the hosepipe for that, in the evening I am forced to use mains water and a watering-can. I timed myself this evening and to my surprise it took me one and a half hours. I do them properly, ensuring that the total volume of compost is wet, so I should not have to do them again for a few days.

*

10 June

I worked for a short time in the garden, dead-heading the Welsh poppies so that they will continue to flower. Then I planted out my sweet corn in the vegetable garden. The variety I have picked this year is an F1 hybrid, which gives quick germination, called 'Extra Tender and Sweet'. I have grown my leeks from seeds using the variety 'Musselburgh Improved', which is derived from an old variety and is very hardy, so it will stay in the ground during the winter without deteriorating.

I then took Tara down by the river for our usual walk, which I enjoyed, and we ended up at Reg and Pat's for a cup of tea.

*

11 June

I left the house early to drive up to Bardills Garden Centre in Nottingham to spend the day answering questions and giving advice on plant selection.

I was asked lots of questions about drought-resistant plants, and my suggested plants included helianthemum, sedum, thymus, diascia, artemisia, nepeta, ballota, eryngium, euphorbia, libertia and the many penstemons.

154

People were still buying lots of bedding plants and were asking about plant combinations for window-boxes and containers. What I tend to do with this type of question is establish what colours the person likes and then fit the plants to the request, mixing foliage colour with flowers. In this way, when the flowering plants have a break, the foliage will carry the interest.

Questions came my way about the hardiness of tropical plants such as banana, palms, cannas and tree ferns. This is a difficult question to answer as hardiness relates to several factors. One is size: in general the larger the plant, the hardier. If the plant is growing in well-drained soil it will survive better than having its feet in water or poorly drained soil, which results in rotting. Position in the garden is also important: a sheltered spot by one side of a doorway may be different from the other side of the doorway. Often plants originating high up a mountain will be hardier than those from sea level. I prefer to over-winter plants in a soil-based compost, such as John Innes, with grit added, rather than coir- or peat-based composts that can sit too wet.

In practice I often say it's a case of try it and see. Giving winter protection, such as wrapping the plant in fleece, will help, as does standing a container on feet, so that if it does freeze, when it starts to thaw the water can drain from the pot. Placing the plant in a sheltered position also helps to ensure the plant will survive. In practice it depends on very local conditions. I have had plants on one side of the garden survive while those on the other die! Sometimes giving advice isn't easy.

In the evening I went to Beaconsfield to hear

three choirs sing. My friend Penny's daughter was in one of the choirs, so it was nice to see her perform. There was a male voice choir, a female voice choir and a mixed choir, and the programme was pleasantly varied.

The concert was held in the open and I do enjoy these outdoor events. There is something very relaxing about sitting outdoors in the sunshine having a picnic surrounded by lovely parkland and then listening to good music with the softness of a summer's evening wind gently caressing you.

*

12–13 June

These days were spent working in my garden and being filmed as I did so. I had thirty-nine 75-litre bags of multipurpose compost delivered so that I could mulch my beds. This means covering the soil with a blanket of compost to prevent water loss through evaporation. I would normally have used fine composted bark, but I couldn't find anyone locally to deliver that amount without a substantial delivery charge, so I went for the compost. I was looking for a small enough particle size to prevent the water evaporating.

My experience has shown that if you use coarse bark the water can escape much more easily than when the particles are close together.

I then stripped the largest of my beds and started to plant it up. This bed is going to be pink, rose and magenta, with the odd bit of purple and white in it. The plants I am using are *Cosmos bipinnatus* in pink and white, purple *Verbena bonariensis*, *Agrostemma githago* in pinks and a few whites, pink geraniums and *Nicotiana* x *hybrida* 'Tinkerbell', a tobacco plant that has dusky-rose petals with lime green on the reverse. At the front of the border I have planted some *Godetia grandiflora* and some small bedding verbenas. Rupert and the gang were fascinated to learn that I never have a formal plan in my head. I normally just stand there with all the plants laid out for planting and then pop them in where they feel right to me.

I obviously think about height distribution throughout the border, which doesn't just mean putting all the taller plants at the back and the shorter ones at the front. I consider the texture of the foliage, so that I have contrast in appearance and habit, and I think about the flower shape. I am trying to play each plant off against its neighbour, so I maximize the effect of all the plants in the border.

I used water-retaining gel in all of the planting holes and had already spread slow-release fertilizer over the whole bed before I started planting. As the afternoon progressed it got darker and darker, and I was hopeful of a storm, as this would save me watering in over 200 plants. I know this sounds like a lot, but I always plant at such a density to prevent weed growth. I believe that the leaves of the plants should shade out the sun and light from around each other so they act as living mulch. I had just got the very last plant in when thunder, lightning and monsoon-like rain stopped play! I dashed indoors and just stood there enjoying the rain and knowing, on this occasion, that enough of it would fall for me not to have to worry about the watering.

*

14–15 June

I woke in an excited mood, as today I was going to *Gardeners' World Live*. Not as a visitor but as a celebrity! This is the first time I had been invited to take part in this event and felt it a privilege to be there. I gave eight presentations during the two days. Four were in the Celebrity Theatre, talking about myself and the making of *Christine's Garden*, and four about 'colour throughout the year' in the Let's Grow Theatre. I had several press engagements, talked to various radio stations, gave magazine interviews and even a website wanted to chat to me.

I enjoyed the two days a lot, and I had a good laugh with the audience when discussing the making of *Christine's Garden*. The other thing that made everyone laugh was my answer to the question 'How do you control slugs in your garden?' I know it's not very PC, but my reply was that I cut them in half with a pair of secateurs or lay them on the path and stand on them. Let's face it, 12 and a half stone of Walkden standing on you is a pretty quick way to go!

I will sometimes use slug pellets, when I have planted something out that is small, or I know is attractive to slugs, but I use them at the recommended application rate (see 25 May). As I've said, most people sprinkle them down like pepper—so thickly that they don't work very well. Used at that rate they are actually unattractive to slugs, which will weave their way through the mine-field of pellets and get to the plant.

I will also use the biological control for slugs and

snails, nematodes, and find them successful, providing you put them on when the soil temperature is high enough and there is enough moisture present for them to work.

I had invited Reg, Pat, Louise and Colin to the first day, and it was lovely to see them all being spoken to by visitors to the show. Reg got asked for his autograph all day long, which he enjoyed, but he sometimes looked slightly embarrassed when asked by ladies if they could have their photograph taken with him. What pleases me so much is the fact that he really enjoys this attention, in the main. In fact the whole gang do.

The other really nice thing, for me, was that so many past students, friends, people for whom I have carried out consultancies, work colleagues and people with whom I had been at college over 30 years ago, turned up to support me during my celebrity spots. I was very moved by this and, of course, happy to meet up with people whom I have not seen in years. They all commented on the fact that it was nice to see me doing well and being successful after all those years of hard work. I must admit that I do believe I have worked very hard over the years, and have never had anything given to me on a silver plate!

At the end of the first day we all stayed the night at a friend of Louise's, and in the evening it was great hearing the chatter of comments on the show, what people had said about *Christine's Garden*, who had said what to Reg and what they all thought of my contributions. This was interesting for me, as it occurred to me that Louise and Reg had never actually seen me working before! Apart from filming with me in the garden they had never seen me doing anything professionally.

We all sat around a large table, enjoying a lovely meal which Jane (Louise's friend) had cooked, and sank a few bottles of wine, and then a few of us moved on to the whisky. Reg and I are both partial to a wee dram, and it finished off the evening a treat, so much nicer than having to stay in an impersonal hotel, often on your own, and eating a meal on your own. I can't say I go a bundle on hotels; it's far nicer to be invited to friends where you can relax and enjoy being together.

*

16–17 June

I came home and back to earth, literally, mulching the borders with compost. This is time-consuming, as I do not wish to bury any plants. The aim, when I mulch, is to keep an even layer of compost about 8cm (3 inches) thick over the border.

With some of the larger plants, that have been in the ground a long time, I will sprinkle some compost into the centre of the plant to encourage the stem bases to root. This helps keeps the plant vigorous and flowering well.

I later spent some time working on the master plan for the horticultural unit I am designing for the Rose Bridge High School in Wigan. This exciting project has to provide facilities, not only for the schoolchildren to use but also for their families and the community if they wish to get involved. Part of my brief is to have an area where the children can build different show gardens, using hard landscaping materials.

To encourage wildlife on to the site, I would like to get the children to surround the show gardens with different hedging plants, some of which will be native to the area. The children will then also gain an understanding of the many techniques that can be used to cut a hedge, such as mechanical hedge trimmer, hand-held shears or secateurs.

The Headmaster is also keen to see honey being produced on the site, so I will allow space for a number of hives. The bees will help with pollination of crops, such as peas and beans, and also in the orchard. I am hoping that the orchard will include varieties of apples, plums and pears etc. which are disappearing from commercial fruit farms in Lancashire.

Six raised beds about 9 sq metres (30 sq feet) square will be used to produce vegetables, along with a polythene tunnel which will allow tomatoes, cucumbers and non-hardy plants to be started off in the early part of spring. I am hopeful that the tunnel will also provide facilities for the children to raise their own plants and grow these on until harvest. I have included some traditional frames next to the polythene tunnel so that the site has somewhere to harden off the young plants before they are planted out in the spring.

18–19 June
I drove up to stay with friends in Newnham, Northamptonshire. They were having a dinner party for several of their friends who had seen *Christine's Garden* and were interested in meeting me. It was a great event, which started at midday

and finished about 5.30 p.m., with lots of great food, wine, port and cheese—everything that I enjoy. We discussed politics without any animosity, world travel (most of us sitting at the table had seen a lot of the world), mutual friends and, of course, the thrills and spills during the making of the programme. We had a great time and spent most of the day laughing.

The following morning, Deirdre and Edgar took me back to see a garden that they had taken me to in April last year, Woodpeckers, near Bidford-on-Avon. This is a plantsman's garden planted to create colour reflecting the changes throughout the year. The herbaceous borders were starting to take on their summer colour, and the roses looked great. What does impress me about this garden is the owner Lallie has an ability to blend shades of the same colour together. Her use of shades of purple, plum, pink and off-white is inspirational.

Both Lallie and her husband, Andy, also have a good eye for using architectural features effectively in the garden. I just love the combination of the formal lines of a millstone against the lines of trimmed box plants growing in terracotta pots. I love visiting gardens, you always come away having learned something new, and often have the chance to pick up a good plant or a cutting.

On this occasion Lallie gave me a cutting of a crassula hybrid I love called *Crassula ovata* 'Hummel's Sunset'. I had made the comment to Lallie that I had not seen this plant for a very long time. She then said she had a cutting and would I like it. This is what gardening is all about.

In my own garden I have many plants

and cuttings that people have given me over the years. When I am there I am surrounded by friends, memories of garden visits, countries explored, places shared, learning experiences, memories of people now gardening in the vast garden in the sky and, of course, shared knowledge, experience and information.

✳

20–21 June

I went up to Wigan with the film crew. They wanted to film me presenting my plan and proposals to the headmaster of Rose Bridge High School.

I had wondered if all involved with this project would be happy with my suggestions. I had prepared rough plans so that, if anything needed changing, this could be done. I presented my proposals to Jack Pendlebury, the headmaster, Bernard from Myerscough College, Vicky the learning manager at the school and two of the children, Tony and Holly, who will be involved with the horticultural unit for the next four years while at school.

They all seemed very happy with what I had suggested, and Holly made a very useful contribution by asking if I'd thought about wildlife. I told her that I had planned for the hedges around the possible show gardens to be planted up with different native plants, with the attraction of wildlife in mind.

One of the things I am keen to develop in the children is an awareness about fresh produce, and have suggested to them that they try and grow enough produce, so that they can either go to a farmers' market and sell what they have produced there, or possibly run a farmers' market on the school site.

I am a great believer in showing reality to children, and have mentioned to the school that I would like the children to be aware of issues to do with growing food, as far as they can understand them. For example, why should you buy from a farmers' market, and why don't more people do this? How should you prepare for a market? Why is customer care and service important? What communication skills do you need? How should you go about selling fresh produce? What are the different styles of selling? How should the produce be displayed? What are the common faults seen in displays? How do you get repeat orders? How do you deal with customer complaints and legal issues such as labels, weights and measures and packaging?

I have made the suggestion that we take the children to a farmers' market so they can see for themselves what they are about.

Once we had completed our discussion, I went outside with the children, who showed me how the crops were growing. They told me that they thought the lettuce was ready for cutting. I asked them if they knew when it was ready and they all said no. I showed them how to tell by applying a slight pressure with the back of the hand to a soft leaf type. If the resistance is there, it's ready. Once we had established which were ready for cutting, I went to cut the first one, only to find it had already been cut. When I asked who had cut it, one of the lads said he had done it, and I had spoiled their plan. He told me that the children had wanted to cut the very first lettuce they themselves produced, and then give it to me.

I was very touched by this gesture! I then said to them that I was going to share it with them. As it was raining, the lettuce had already been washed so I cut the centre out, unpeeled individual leaves and we all shared it together. I also explained that they would never ever get another opportunity to taste their first lettuce again. I asked them what they thought, and they said they liked it.

What was very nice for me was to see these children take their first lettuce home with them. I would have loved to be a fly on the wall in some of their homes just to hear what the parents said.

During the time that I was being filmed, Andy, the assistant headmaster, was taking photographs of the interactions between me and the children. At one stage he was walking backwards, so he could get us all in shot, when, all of a sudden, he disappeared down a ditch. Everyone started laughing until they realized that Andy had not resurfaced. Several people ran over to the ditch, only to find Andy up to his knees in water, having slid down the ditch backwards. Fortunately, the only thing that was hurt was his pride!

On returning home, I took some spare tomato plants round to Reg. I had saved him two 'Sungold' plants, which I know Pat likes more than the 'Alicante' that Reg is growing this year, and two plants of 'Snow White Cherry', which I have not tried either. I obtained the seed from the Heritage Seed Library at Garden Organic. They describe them as being similar to 'Gardener's Delight' but with yellow flesh instead of red.

*

22 June

I decided to transplant my leeks. I always give them a good watering before lifting them to protect the roots. I had sown them fairly thinly, but they were now the thickness of a pencil, so they needed more room.

Because my soil is very light and contains a lot of sand, if I try making a hole with a dibber, when I remove the dibber the soil just quickly runs back into the hole and fills it. I have also tried taking out individual holes, about 13cm (5 inches) deep, but that takes for ever when I am replanting about 200 leeks.

The technique that I have found works best is to water the soil really well so that it is damp to about 15cm (6 inches) deep. I then place a line down so that I plant in a straight row. I push the spade blade into the soil against the line and just pull the spade forward to give me a slit. The leeks are placed in the slit, at about 10cm (4 inches) apart, and then the soil is watered back into place.

I like leeks very much and will eat them raw as well as cooked, so, once they get to a reasonable size, I will start to harvest some and use them like spring onions; I leave the rest for use over the winter.

In the evening I went over to college to work with my students on their plots. They carried out general maintenance—weeding, removing side shoots from their tomato plants, tying in the sweet peas, hoeing through their annual borders—and generally just ensured that the plots were looking neat and tidy.

*

23–24 June
These were a couple of days spent doing all sorts of bits and pieces.

My brother, sister-in-law and niece came to spend the night with me on their way to Heathrow airport to see my niece, Sarah, off for three months' work in America. Sarah is developing a love of travelling, which pleases me, as I do not feel that we have that much in common. I told her about countries I had visited, and we talked about what should she expect from her visit to America.

Once they had all left, I put together yet another compost bin. This makes my fourth. I am a great believer that you cannot have enough compost. My light soil digests compost, and organic matter, at such a great rate that I never have enough, and am always on the look out for a cheap source of suitable material.

A past garden design student of mine had phoned to say that she had a supply of partly rotted horse manure, so I asked if she could deliver me a load. Getting this up the garden was remarkably hard work. My garden slopes up away from the house at the back and there is a 2.7-m (9-foot) height difference from the front of the house, where the manure was dropped, to the top of the garden, where it was put in the new compost bin, ready for the late autumn or winter when I carry out my winter digging. I had to get it up a flight of steps, about 1m (3 feet) high, and then barrow it up to the vegetable garden, and into a compost bin which is 1.2m (4 feet) tall. I was very tired and aching by the time I had finished.

I am always keen to meet up with friends and past students, but at the moment time seems to be passing at such a rate it's untrue, and I'm under a lot of pressure to get on with work, having several deadlines to meet. However, I feel it's very important to maintain contact with people and friends. After all, it is people that really matter in life, so I decided to accept an invitation to go out for a meal with some of my past students.

We spent the evening talking about the things they have been doing since leaving college, which included gardening and garden design. We then moved on to chatting about the first series of *Christine's Garden*. I find it fascinating that people took such a variety of different things from the series. I find that some people will say they enjoyed the banter between Reg and me; some mentioned my walks down by the river with Tara, while others liked my eating the tomatoes, and other vegetables, and obviously enjoying them so much. Some people comment that it was a gardener sharing her garden with them in a very normal way that they could relate to; some say it was the poetic moments that they enjoyed and shared, while others tell me that they cried when I did!

One of my students said that the bit that meant most to her was when I went up to see my old lecturer, Ben Andrews, in Garstang, after 32 years. She said it was the relationship that I had with him, and the things that he had given to me, which were now being passed on to her, and all my other students. She encouraged me to continue giving my knowledge, passion, humour and enthusiasm to students, as she thought I was inspirational. I do find handling such comments difficult. I am not used to being complimented, so am never really sure what I should say apart from 'thank you'!

*

25 June

I started the day by taking down the winter hanging baskets and taking out any of the old plants that could be kept. This included the polyanthus, *Euphorbia* 'Redwing' and the *Erysimum* 'Stars and Stripes'. These old plants have now been planted in the borders. I then hung up my summer flowering baskets, which include a rather traditional mix of petunias, fuchsias, variegated geraniums, lobelias, busy lizzies, nemesia, verbena and helichrysum. These had been planted up now for about three weeks, but the winter baskets had been looking so good I did not want to take them down. However, now they had started to look tired, so down they came and the new ones are up in their place.

Several of my houseplants had roots growing out of the bottom of the pots, which is a sure sign that they need moving on into a bigger pot. I repotted those that needed doing. This gives the root system more room and also provides some fresh food for the plants, so will give then a lift.

Most of my aeoniums, which I have over-wintered in the living-room behind the dining-room table, have been moved outside for the summer, and the really leggy ones have been started again by taking cuttings. This is very simple,

169

all you do is remove the growing point of the plant with about 2.5cm (1 inch) of stem and pot it into some gritty, soil-based compost with about half as much course grit added. I then throw the old leggy plant away.

I then went into the vegetable garden to harvest my 'Mange tout' peas and some lettuce. I had so many peas that I nipped round to Reg and Louise with some for each of them. I got into Reg's only to find that Pat was serving me up a lovely lunch. My timing could not have been better. Reg had apparently been knocking at my front door, but I hadn't heard him as I was at the top of the garden harvesting the peas! What was nice about this surprise was the fact that the potatoes, carrots and broad beans, which accompanied the roast lamb, were all out of Reg's garden, followed by his raspberries. It was a happy interlude to my day.

In the afternoon I took Tara down to the river for a walk. I love this walk, and the countryside changes on a weekly basis. The fields are now covered with plantains sending up their thin flower spikes. Only a month ago the cow parsley, or—to use one of its other common names, which I prefer—Queen Ann's Lace, was in flower. A fortnight previously the same fields were covered in buttercups, and even earlier, dandelions.

I also love watching the sky scapes; the clouds and light change so much. I often feel like an artist is painting in front of me as I walk. The rippling grasses, the reflections in the river when it is calm, the sounds of the birds, the wind in my face all give me such pleasure and a feeling that it's good to be alive. How lucky I am to be able to appreciate all this beauty around me.

A lot of people think that Essex and Hertfordshire are not very nice places to live, what with the many building developments and also Stansted airport. However, as is the case in every county in the United Kingdom without exception, I could show you places that would make you appreciate that this common thought is so far from the truth, it's silly.

At dinner-time Louise knocked on the front door and asked if I would like to join them for dinner. I explained that I had enjoyed such a good lunch with Reg and Pat that I was still feeling full! It's lovely to have this sort of relationship with the neighbours. I think they all know that, being on my own, I very seldom cook a traditional Sunday meal. However, they know how much I enjoy it, and, of course, it's just so nice to be sitting at a table enjoying each other's company rather than eating on my own.

*

26 June

For the first time in a long time, it has rained, gently, all day and I am so very pleased. The soil, at depth, is very dry, so a steady gentle rainfall will do a lot of good. The hose-pipe ban is still in force and, even with a pump for the bath-water, watering the containers on and around the patio is a time-consuming job.

I decided to spend the day in the office catching up with the post, e-mails, telephone calls and preparing for teaching this week and for courses that I am due to present next week. I am also preparing to interview candidates for a gardener's job at the Kirklees Light Railway. I must say that paperwork is not my favourite pastime, but it is all part of the job. I do, however, enjoy preparing material for teaching and training, as I like to ensure I will meet the objectives of the day.

In the evening I went over to Chelmsford to give one of my students some advice on her garden. Dawn has been trying to get it looking good for a number of years, but she felt it just was not coming together. We wandered round together and had a really good look, and then I suggested that one of her major problems was that all of the borders were too narrow, which results in difficulty achieving a sense of balance, and a good distribution of heights and shapes throughout the border.

The next problem was up in Dawn's vegetable area. She wanted advice on how many apple trees to plant to divide the vegetable area from the rest of the garden. I said it very much depended on which rootstock she chooses and then recommended using either M7 or M9, which will not grow tall, but will start to fruit quickly. She was undecided about which varieties she should choose, and I said the real thing to watch was that they could pollinate each other, and to seek advice from the nursery.

We then moved to the front of the house where a row of conifers are growing, but many of them are looking brown and sick. Upon inspection, it was obvious that they were going brown from the outside inwards, which indicates lack of water. The other situation that often occurs with conifers is that they go brown from the inside outwards. This normally indicates insect damage caused by the conifer-spinning mite. Just to make sure all was OK within the plant, I cut away a bit of the bark about 10cm (4 inches) up from the ground on the stem to check that there was no staining in the plant's plumbing system (the phloem and xylem). The stem was revealed to be nice and green and moist, indicating that all was well. I suggested that she tried to give then more water, if she could.

I stayed and had supper with Dawn and her husband. This consisted of roast beef, and all the trimmings, which was a lovely way of rewarding me for my advice!

*

27 June

I went to my client in Epping Forest and, again, spent most of the day weeding paths by hand. Brigid is very careful about using anything in the garden that may possibly upset the birds and foxes she feeds on the paths. I must say that weeding by hand is time-consuming and monotonous but, if that is what she would like me to do, I respect her wishes.

In the evening I went over to college and worked with my students on the plots. We harvested the first courgettes, weeded through the beds and then spent much of the rest of the time weeding their annual borders and replacing any plants which had died or were just looking very weak.

The sweet peas have started to flower, so we picked these in the hope of keeping them flowering. The problem we have with these plots is they are not watered regularly and now things are looking extremely dry. I am not sure that they will continue flowering over the summer holidays. I suspect they will just go to seed.

*

28–29 June

I had a good drive up to the Kirklees Light Railway at Clayton West. It took four hours but was not a difficult trip; it's just a long way from home. I do, however, enjoy seeing the different counties I drive through—Cambridgeshire, Bedfordshire, Northamptonshire, Leicestershire, Derbyshire and then into Yorkshire. I enjoy seeing the countryside change, noticing the varying densities of trees and the different types of hedgerows and shrubs growing alongside the roads, and watching the scenery become more undulating.

The main reason for the visit was to carry out interviews for the position of gardener. The owners of the site had had a good response to the advertisement for the position and knew the type of person they needed, but didn't feel expert enough on gardening to know exactly what they were looking for, or to interpret modern horticultural qualifications.

I enjoy interviewing for staff, as it is an opportunity to find out about a person's life. I admit it's a bit artificial, but I enjoy chatting to people and seeing what they have done with their lives and what their aspirations are. I am also always surprised how little preparation some people give to this important situation; after all, it could be a life-changing move. Some of the candidates had never even visited the site beforehand! Bearing in mind that it's a public visitor attraction, I would have thought the first thing you would have done is visit to see what actually was involved.

In the end I went for a chap who seemed well suited to the position. He was enthusiastic, had been to the site before and had even been there on the planting day that I carried out with the local schoolchildren, but had not made himself known to me at the time. It did show that he was interested enough to come and see what I was up to. He also brought along to the interview photographs of his past work and projects. This was not only nice to see, but actually proved that he had done what he was talking about. I am hopeful that he will integrate well with the other staff and will enjoy the work.

I spent the rest of my time trying to organize the requirements for a master-class in hanging basket making for any volunteers who would like to be involved. My hope is that we can get between 40 and 50 people.

There, I will demonstrate how to make a basket and then let them have a go. All the materials, and the plants, will be provided for them. I am hopeful that we may get groups of people working together to plant a basket. They will then be hung on the front of the station building and will be looked after, during the summer, by the volunteers and the newly appointed gardener. I think it would be nice if, in late September or October, we were to invite a garden expert from a local radio station to come and judge the best one and give out a prize.

The other thing I did was to meet up with Andy Whittle, the environmental officer for the Denby

Dale Countryside Project. The railway is on his patch, so he was keen to meet me and see what my plans were for developing the line and site. He seemed greatly relieved when I told him that it is my intention to keep to native plants along the railway line and not to bring in exotic material which would destroy a bit of native Yorkshire.

He did say that he was worried that I am a horticulturist rather than an environmentalist. He thought I would want to make it all pretty and pay little regard to what was already there. I went on to explain that, though I trained as a horticulturist, I spend much of my time travelling and photographing wild places around the world and am hugely respectful of natural habitats and all that they represent. I said that I had plans to make the car park and front of the site look much more attractive and, horticulturally, more interesting, but was not about to destroy something that I believe is very rare these days—a green corridor. This is somewhere where the habitat has not been altered over many years, so that the wildlife and flowers are rich and diverse, unlike most open countryside these days, due to modern farming practice.

The other chap I spent time with was the managing director of the PR company that the owners are using to promote the site and deal with the programme of events. This was a useful meeting, as I was able to express my feelings about the site, and what I wished to achieve over a five-year period. We also spoke about possible PR opportunities while I was up visiting the site and how to make sure that we all operate within the guidelines which the BBC set for this type of activity. I am keen to try and keep everyone happy in all that I do, and am aware of the press opportunities that could be gained from my involvement with the railway, but have no intention of causing problems in relation to the new series and the BBC.

As the owners were not on the site while I was there, I produced a written report for them before I left. I wanted them to be aware of what I had done, whom I had appointed and what I would like to see done before my next visit.

30 June

Back at home I found that my garden was looking very dry so I decided to water it using the bath-water. This is an extremely funny operation on your own, as really it is a two-man job. Firstly, I have to get the hose-pipe up into the bathroom. This is done by putting a washing line through the window and then attaching the hose to it and pulling the hose up. Because the end of the hosepipe needs to be under the water for me to be able to syphon the water out, I use a brick to weigh it down. This partly restricts the size of the pipe opening. I then go downstairs and suck madly on the end of the hose! Eventually I get a mouthful of bathwater and off I go. I suppose I am lucky that at least it is my own dirty water and not someone else's!

The other method I've mentioned before is to carry buckets of the water down the stairs, but it takes ages and is very hard work.

In the afternoon I spent time writing my weekly articles and then packed all I need for a garden tour of Sussex and Surrey which I am leading over the next three days. In the evening I took Tara over to Elaine and Phil's. Tara is always so happy to see them and be with them that I think she thinks of them as her other family. They do look after her so well and love her as much as their own dog.

JULY

1–3 July

I drove down to Abingworth Hall, in West Sussex, to lead a garden tour of Sussex and Surrey over the next three days. I arrived in time for the normal meeting with the manager of the hall. I had never met her before, but I soon realized we would get on like a house on fire. She had a great sense of humour. We discussed the logistics of my tour, what I would be doing with the group in the evenings, and which rooms I would be able to use. I was then left to welcome the guests as they arrived.

I find it interesting to meet people when they have travelled any distance. Generally, they are not at their best then, and I have now learned to reserve any judgements about them until well into the second day. On arrival, people are tired, and often feeling apprehensive about where they are going and worrying about what their rooms, the food and the other guests will be like and, very importantly, what the leader will be like! All in all, not the best terms under which to gain first impressions. Sometimes a person who's grumpy or difficult on arrival can change completely after a night's sleep and turn out to be the life and soul of the party.

We all joined together for the evening meal and then I led a brief meeting with introductions all round. I talked to them about the way I run tours, as well as timings and arrangements for meals, before having a general chat to people about their own gardens.

179

I had printed off a weather forecast for the duration of the tour and I was alarmed to see that it was going to be over 30°C (86°F) the whole time. I enjoy temperatures in the twenties but, once it gets above this I feel distinctly uncomfortable. I asked everyone to ensure they had plenty of water with them during our visits.

Garden tours tend to attract older people, so I was aware that the group would need to take it very steady in such heat. In practice everyone managed really well and even I had no problems.

Because West Sussex, like Essex, had very little rain over the winter, unfortunately the trees and shrubs were looking quite stressed, with thin heads and wilting young growth. The rest of the plants, and lawns, also looked very tired, so people were not seeing the lovely gardens at their best.

The roses at Polesden Lacey, near Dorking, in Surrey, were looking fine, but the other herbaceous plants were wilting in the heat. A lot of the group decided they would complete the tree walk and then go inside the house in order to keep out of the sun.

Sir Fredrick Stern's garden, Highdown, has a fantastic collection of unusual trees, and some of these were lovely, as were the climbing roses growing all over several trees and shrubs. Some of the party stayed with me for the afternoon, instead of going off and doing their own thing, and we spent a very pleasant hour sitting together on benches in the shade, chatting about the plants we had seen, how to propagate these and our own gardens.

After dinner I offered the group the opportunity to ask me questions. This was a fascinating session.

I was not asked the normal things that come up in a gardeners' question time. The subjects that did come up, and we discussed, included: the value of seed banks, such as the one at Wakehurst Place, where I once worked, the purpose of seed banks (are they only for flowers?), the role of botanic gardens in conservation, the costs involved in maintaining a garden open to the public, and then routine things like plant identifications, how to control slugs, how to control ground elder and so on.

The following morning we went off to Munstead Wood, near Godalming, in Surrey. I had been several times before, but had never been around the house. When I was arranging the visit, Lady Clark asked me if I would like to see the house with my group. I said yes straight away.

Munstead Wood was the home of the famous gardener and artist, Gertrude Jekyll. Her house had been built by Edwin Lutyens in 1896. Unfortunately, it contained little from that period, although we were shown the original Lutyens design. It was fascinating to be taken through the house by Lady Clark, however, and see the inside.

The gardener then took us on a tour of the garden. Unfortunately, the heat was having a bad affect, and again the garden did not look its best. The season has also been very late, so we were in between things. It was a pity, as these gardens are really fantastic when all the rhododendrons and magnolias are out.

The final visit was to High Beeches. I used to visit it ages ago when I was working at Wakehurst Place. What a change—better visitor facilities, and also a wider range of plants and trees than I remember. It is a steep garden in places, and I did wonder how some of the party would cope, but everyone managed really well and saw some very spectacular *Cornus kousa* in full flower. In fact two of the trees were covered with so many flowers that you could not see the leaves.

✻

4 July
The day was spent up at Jesus College, Cambridge, teaching some of their staff, plus staff from other Cambridge colleges, about pruning.

I always welcome comment during my training sessions, but the morning theoretical period was fairly heavy going. It became very obvious that at least two people in the room did not wish to be there. I do find this situation frustrating, as I would rather someone didn't come, than that they put a damper on things for the others. One of the two came round very quickly, once I split them up into groups for some of the exercises, but the other chap was actually rude.

At the break I did speak to his team leader, who said he had also noticed the man's manner and would have a chat with him at lunch-time. This he did, whereupon the man responded that he knew all there was to know about pruning and the course was beneath him!

After lunch, we went into the grounds to carry out a practical session, reflecting what they had discussed and learned during the morning session. The difficult student showed little respect for any plants, often just walking on them, or throwing his tools on the ground, and had very little idea of how to prune correctly. I had to speak to him several times during the afternoon.

At the end of the day I spoke to the head gardener and reported the situation to him. I never like leaving a site, after a training session, if I think it hasn't all gone in the way I wished. He noted my observations, expressed some interesting comments of his own about the chap and then thanked me for a good day. Others on the course had spoken positively, saying they had enjoyed both sessions and had got a lot out of the day.

5 July

I spent the day completing the mulching of my garden. I was working on the largest of the borders, which is about 3m (10 feet) square in size, when Rupert and the gang turned up wanting to film this.

Filming always makes any job much longer. Rupert is a first-rate director who is 'self shooting'—this means that he is using the camera as a cameraman as well as directing what we are doing. He has a fantastic eye for detail, but this means that things need to be recorded several times from several different angles. I initially thought that it was me, always doing things wrong, but have learned, over time, that while sometimes it is me, often it's because of the wrong light or the wrong angle or for one of many other technical reasons that he is asking me to do it over and over again.

What was odd about the day was that, as soon as I had finished putting on the last handful of compost, the heavens opened and we had a tremendous thunderstorm. I had just said to the camera, 'What I could do with now is a good downpour'! Well, someone was listening. The rain kept up for about three hours. It could not have been better.

However, what was really odd was that the last time we did any filming on this bed, the time when I planted it up, exactly the same thing happened. I had finished planting, and said those famous words 'I could do with a downpour', when we had a similar thunderstorm. It was all a bit uncanny.

In the evening Rupert and Sarah invited me round to the house they are renting for the duration of filming, for a meal and to look at where we are in the series and what we need for the rest of filming.

This is a fascinating process, as I have no idea how much of what they have filmed can be used in the final programme. Rupert carries the story-lines in his head, but does not want to share them with me, as he enjoys the spontaneous nature of my comments. He is constantly saying that the less I think about something, the better it is! He would rather film me saying something for the very first time.

We do not always agree on what he wants. This is usually to do with his asking me to wait a while before doing something in the garden, so that he can film it. Unfortunately, plants don't wait for camera crews.

None of the crew is a gardener, and at times this leads to frustration. They do not realize that a week can be far too long to wait for something to be filmed. Flowers can go over in just a few days, seeds need to be sown at a certain time and jobs have to be carried out when I have the time, and energy, to do them. Filming is not the only thing in my life. Sometimes I will agree, but my garden and plants are worth far more to me than any TV series.

My garden is my sanctuary. It's where I can do what I want, how I want. I do not have to conform to anyone and that's what I enjoy about it.

A lot of my professional life is spent meeting exacting targets, fulfilling high levels of expectation in a world where you have to be correct and up-to-date. I do not have a problem with this, but, when I'm back at home, I do not like having constraints put on me!

*

6 July

I started the day by pruning the *Magnolia* x *soulangeana* that grows in my front garden. By this time of the year, it has put on long thin shoots of growth that need cutting back to help develop flowering buds for next spring. I take all the shoots back to two leaves from the main stem, using secateurs, and I always congratulate myself in the spring when it flowers so well.

Three years ago I reduced the height considerably, to make it manageable. It means I can prune it from a step ladder, even though I still have to stand on the top step. At the end I collect all the prunings, grind them up and put them on my compost heap.

During the afternoon Sarah, the Assistant Producer for the second series, phoned me to arrange filming dates and asked what I had been

185

up to during the morning. I mentioned to her that I had pruned the magnolia. Within five minutes Rupert was on the phone telling me off! He said that he had been featuring the magnolia every time they filmed the front of the house. This enabled them to match that day's filming with the rest of the material they film during that day and is a cheaper, and better, method than trying to 'grade scenes' which involves ensuring that the light levels and colours match when different sections of filming are cut and edited.

Rupert said it made things difficult for him when I do things without telling him. I explained that I did not realize there was a problem, because, when we had discussed pruning Reg's magnolia, he had not seemed particularly interested, so I assumed he was not interested in seeing mine done! Rupert never told me he was featuring it, so how the heck was I supposed to know! I find this lack of communication frustrating and annoying. I don't want to make things difficult for him, but I need to get jobs done at the correct time.

In the evening I drove down to the Millbrook Garden Centre to give one of my most popular lectures—'How to grow 2,000 plants in a 20 x 30 foot garden'. In this talk I look at alpines, dwarf shrubs, growing plants in sinks, walls, paving, hanging baskets, raised towers and beds, under-planting of borders with deciduous shrubs (those that lose their leaves for the winter) and the use of tufa, a soft rock in which you can actually grow plants.

The lecture was well received and there seemed to be a lot of laughter, which was nice. I try to make my talks light-hearted and funny as well as educational. I must come out with some very funny things, judging by the audience's response, but I am not always aware of what I have just said! Sometimes, when the laughter is prolonged, I wish I could recall my own remarks!

7 July

I spent another day, on my knees, weeding Brigid's crazy paving patio and paths, by hand.

I have seen a family of foxes playing in the garden, and I must say it's a sheer delight to see the male and female play with their four little ones in broad daylight. It makes all the time-consuming effort seem worthwhile. I must say that, at the end of the day, I have a job straightening up, and my knees give me hell for a couple of days. I could always say no, but I respect Brigid's wishes and the job only needs doing two to three times a year.

8 July

I cut the hedge between next door and myself. This is a *Cotoneaster lacteus* hedge, which produces long new shoots by this time in the year. These I remove individually with secateurs. If I use a mechanical hedge trimmer, it cuts the large leaves in half, which then dry out and turn brown, making the whole thing look very unsightly.

Next I rearranged all the pots and containers that sit at the base of the hedge. Any that needed repotting, such as the golden rain tree, *Koelreuteria paniculata*, some of the bamboos, the Crowborough lily, *Zantedeschia aethiopica* and a collection of what used to be called coleus, but are now called solenostemon, were all moved on into pots one or two sizes larger.

I gave them all a really good soak before repotting them, and then watered them again afterwards. This ensures that the soil is fully wet, and settles the new soil around the rootball, thus avoiding any air spaces, into which the roots cannot grow.

When I rearrange them, I am looking for contrasts in size, shape of plant, foliage, texture and flowering times, so as to maximize the effect of each plant against the others around it.

I had grown some perennial sweet peas from seeds and these were now 15cm (6 inches) tall, so I decided to plant them at the base of the north wall of the house, near my kitchen. Although these sweet peas appreciate a sunny position, I have found that they will also do well against a north-facing wall.

During the evening I spent time writing my weekly gardening articles. I had been working for about an hour and a half when I decided to take a break and nip round to see if Reg, Pat, Louise and Colin were in. I went round to invite them over, tomorrow evening, for a glass of wine and some cheese and biscuits.

I have been so busy this year that I am beginning to feel that I am neglecting them. I often nip over and have a cup of tea, but we have not had an evening together for some time, so I thought that for once I would put work behind me. It will be lovely to spend some time with the people who are

188

important to me.

*

9 July

On waking at 6 a.m., I was still feeling shattered, even after a good night's sleep, so I decided to get back into bed and set the alarm clock for 8 a.m. Well, I was woken, eventually, by a friend phoning me at 10.20. I cannot remember the last time I slept in like that. Even though I have been feeling very tired of late, I am so busy that normally I just get up and get going.

I must admit that there are times when I find it difficult to combine working, obtaining and preparing future work, trying to have a private life and coping with things like shopping, cleaning, etc. I think mostly it's because I live alone. Everything that has to be done has to be done by me! I have no one to ask to help and, sometimes, I feel I am running all of the time but getting nowhere fast.

I decided to take Tara down to the river, and have an hour together enjoying the fields full of yarrow in full bloom. I always find that this walk leaves me feeling better, and I love seeing Tara trot along happily with her tail up. She is getting old now, and cannot go as far as she used to, but we still enjoy our time together.

I spent some time during the afternoon catching up with this diary, it takes up a large part of the day because I only use four fingers to type—when I started writing it was only two!

Reg, Pat, Louise and Colin came round and we had a lovely evening, talking about all sorts of things including Louise's mother's charm bracelet. On it there's a miniature church which, when you open it up, shows the people inside, and a holder for an old-fashioned pound note folded up really small.

Talk of old-fashioned pound notes being folded up reminded me of a story of my father's wedding day. There is a photo of him and my mum, standing outside the church. My dad looks as if he has a large breast on the left-hand side of his chest. It was actually his wallet, brimming with old-fashioned £5 notes that he had folded to get them to fit in. This made it bulge as his suit was a bit too tight for him!

Reg and Pat chatted about the holiday they are hoping to have in Madeira in September. I asked them about where they had been in the past. Reg used to work on the railway and, on his retirement, was given a pass to travel more or less anywhere in Britain and Europe at no, or very little, cost.

Over the years they have had holidays in Italy, Yugoslavia, Greece, Turkey, Monte Carlo and France, but the best of all seems to have been Capri. They said they would like to go back, but, now they are getting older, rail travel and carrying their own suitcases is not so easy for them.

Reg recounted that, in the past, when a train pulled into their station on the continent, he would send one of the family inside to find their carriage and they would push the suitcases in though the window. This was easier than trying to get the cases down the aisle with so many other people trying to do the same thing.

I always enjoy their company. They have had an interesting life and are always willing to recall past times. We normally end up laughing at their remembered adventures.

*

10 July

I spent the vast majority of the day writing, with a break in the afternoon to trim my bay tree to shape. To do this job I used secateurs, which don't damage the leaves. When I took Tara out, I chatted to the farmer down the lane, who had caught an eel from the river the previous day. He made my mouth water at his description of smoking and eating it.

*

11–12 July

I drove over to Buckhurst Hill to prune a hedge for friends. Well, in reality, it is a shrub border that, over the years, has been allowed to grow together, so it's now maintained and pruned like a hedge.

I always look at this job and think I must be mad. The border is at least 18m (60 feet) long, 3m (10 feet) wide and, at the time of pruning, about 3–3.5m (10–12 feet) tall. What makes the job much more time-consuming than it need be is that the owners don't want it cut with an electric hedge trimmer. Noise is an issue, as the hedge surrounds a block of flats, and they also fear that an electric cable stretching over the grass, for about 45m (150 feet), could cause an accident. So I prune it with a pair of secateurs! To add to the fun, the prunings then have to be bagged up.

Rupert and the gang wished to film me doing this job, and found it very funny to see me actually disappear into the hedge so that I could prune the middle. Over the years I have found that it's easier going in underneath to reach the middle than

191

trying to stretch over from a ladder on the outside.

Because it seemed so odd to Rupert, he decided that he would like to view me from the top of the flats, so he asked my friend if he could go on the roof. It was also unusual, from my point of view, having a camera pointing at me from the top of a block of flats while I worked. Time will tell if this bit of footage worked. I will only know when I see it being broadcast.

It was really hard work doing this hedge as the temperature was 35°C (95°F) during the hottest part of the day. The perspiration was rolling off me, and I had to keep stopping to wipe my face as it was getting in my eyes and the salt was stinging.

There was a lot of material to come off this time, and in the end I had to work until 8.30 p.m. to get it finished. Filming always eats time, and what would normally take me about 10 hours, took 18 hours! We needed to get it finished, however. If we had come back to it, light levels would have been different and the hedge would have looked different.

Filming days always have a start time but never an end time. You keep filming until you finish the job, the light goes or the director is happy. Some days can be very long, and on these occasions I always feel extremely done in. I think it's because not only is the physical work demanding, but I am concentrating all day and, even when we are not filming, chatting to people.

I sometimes feel completely empty by the end of the day. I often just have a bath, a snack, because I am too tired to do anything else, and then go to bed.

On days like that none of my other jobs get

done. I have training courses to prepare for, correspondence course students' scripts to mark, consultancies, e-mails to answer, lectures and presentations to prepare, weekly gardening articles to write and, of course, my own garden to maintain.

Filming is fun but other stuff starts to build up. Time seems to be passing at such a speed it's alarming. Just how have we got to the second week of July?

✱

13 July

One of Louise's trees, which we planted together during Series One, suffered a lot of die-back at the top during the winter, so I decided it needed replacing. I took its replacement round and asked Louise to plant it. I was very keen to see if she had remembered the important points to carry out when planting a tree, which I taught her last year.

The tree should be watered well, both before and after planting, and the hole should be 5-8cm (2-3 inches) bigger than the rootball. If the soil is well-drained, some organic matter should be incorporated into the planting hole, and forked into the soil to ensure that it is mixed together. When it's not properly mixed, but just put in as a layer, it can act as a barrier to the tree's roots and stop them growing out into the surrounding soil.

Louise was great, she remembered the lessons. We made sure that the planting depth, in the ground, was the same as the soil level in the pot, by using a spade handle to measure how deep the tree would be sitting when placed in the hole. After a slight adjustment, we took the tree out of the pot and partly back-filled the hole. We did this by mixing some more compost with the soil taken out of the hole, and then, putting in about 23cm (9 inches) of soil before gently firming this and watering well. This allows the soil to settle against the root system. Finally we filled the hole with the remaining soil and gave it a really good watering. In total we had used about 4 gallons of water.

We did not use a stake, as modern research has shown that unstaked trees, providing they are not planted in a very windy site, develop cells in the stem in response to slight movement which make them stronger than if they are staked. My experience, over the past few years, has shown that this method works and does produce a better tree, capable of standing up on its own, far more quickly.

✳

14–15 July
These were very hot days; even with a fan on in the office all day, I find it very difficult to concentrate. I took breaks to go up into the vegetable garden and harvest my runner beans and courgettes, and dig up some of my potatoes. I harvested the last of the peas, pulled the plants out of the ground and composted them. There weren't that many peas, so I ate them raw.

Whenever I eat raw peas I remember the summers spent at my grandmother's. I would nip into her garden, pick the peas and eat them. I was always found out and told off. I liked raw peas so much that, when the mobile greengrocer used to call, I would buy a bottle of dandelion and burdock pop and a bag of peas from him, climb over the fence at the bottom of Granny's garden and sit in the fields eating the peas, drinking the pop and watching the river go by. Oh, what fond childhood memories.

Having harvested the peas, I decided to sow some French beans, radishes and more salad leaves in the free space. Due to the dryness of this summer in this part of the world, I have incorporated a large amount of compost into the soil in the hope that it will act like a sponge and will help to retain the water.

The next crop to be harvested was the broad beans. I have been taking these for the past three weeks, but they are coming to an end, so I decided I would freeze the rest. I do this simply by shelling the pods, washing the beans and placing them in a single layer in the freezer. When they are frozen I bag them up. I never blanch them.

I took lettuces, radishes and some of my runner beans round to Reg and Pat and had a cup of tea with them. They had been into Harlow shopping, but they had found it too hot and came home early to try and get cool.

In the evening, once it had cooled down, I went out and removed faded flowers. This included petunias, cosmos, agrostemma, sweet peas, nicotiana, godetia, rudbeckia, calendula, *Lychnis coronaria* and *Verbena bonariensis*.

If you remove the spent flowers regularly, the plants will go on producing more flowers. If you leave the

195

faded flowers on, and they develop into seeds, the plant thinks it's done its job of reproducing and will not produce more flowers.

*

16 July

I went over to see a couple of friends in Harlow and to meet up with another mutal friend whom we hadn't seen in ages. It was a lovely afternoon, and we all sat in the garden as it was too hot in the house. Our common interest was gardening. Sue was one of my past students, and her sister, Chris, is just starting to garden, while our mutual friend Julie and I worked together when we were at Capel Manor in Enfield. While she was there I introduced her to teaching, so we spent some time talking about recent changes to the RHS courses that we both teach.

Chris presented me with a lovely pineapple lily (eucomis) that she had grown. I have a fascination for South African plants and grow eucomis in the garden. I find that, providing they are planted about 10–15cm (4–6 inches) deep, they survive the winter and come up each year. They do need a warm well-drained soil to over-winter.

In the evening I prepared a new lecture, that I will be giving for the first time next week, entitled 'The Making of *Christine's Garden*'. This is a talk that discusses, amongst other things, the ups and downs associated with spending the summer with three people filming in my home and garden, and on the road while I am working away.

It always surprises me just how long it takes to put an hour's slide presentation together. You have to think about the start, what points you wish to make and which slides you wish to use, then load all the slides into the magazine for the projector and go through it several times to ensure that it will flow properly on the night.

*

17 July

What a hard day this was—at one stage the temperature was over 36°C (100°F) in my garden. Rupert and the gang turned up to film me helping Louise with her garden. She continues to develop it, putting in borders and planting shrubs and perennial plants, which will come up every year.

I went round and asked her what help she wanted. It was the top of the garden that she was bothered about. Nothing will grow under the conifers over-hanging her garden from next door's, and the soil here is full of glass, stones and rubbish, and does not retain any moisture.

I said that if we cut the conifers back to the neighbour's fence that would remove the shade problem. We would then have to remove any glass from the soil and add as much compost as possible. This would help retain moisture.

The first thing that needed to be established was the width of the border she wanted there. She had already drawn a line, but had made the common mistake of marking out a border that was too narrow. As I've said before, this makes it very difficult, when planting the border, to get a distribution of height from the front to the back.

The general rule goes that the highest plant should be half the width of the border. So, if you have a border 2.4m (8 ft) wide, nothing growing in it should be higher than 1.2m (4 ft).

Louise and I marked out the shape of the border using a hosepipe. This is easy to see, and it can be moved around until the desired shape and width have been achieved.

We then went about removing all the weeds and grass. This was incredibly hard work as the heat was overpowering. Jimmy, our soundman, said at one stage that his watch was recording a temperature of 36°C (100°F). We worked until about 3 p.m., when I had to call it a day. Louise had wanted to get this job done, but the heat had got to me and I was well and truly done in. It was also far too hot to even consider doing any digging in of compost and turning over the soil to get it ready for planting, let alone the planting itself.

What we did do, before putting everything away, was to carry out a simple pH test that we had obtained from the garden centre. This showed us that the soil contains lime and therefore there is little point in buying plants that like acid soil conditions.

Since it was so hot we all decided we would have a meal together, so Sarah, who is a fantastic cook, offered to do the cooking for us. I have never worked with an assistant producer who was so into preparing really nice food. It was lovely being able to spend some time together. Normally at the end of a day's filming the crew just pack up their things and disappear until it's time to do more filming.

✳

18 July

The film crew have a production office in Harlow, and I went round to have a chat with them about our filming schedule and what I would be doing over the next few weeks.

It's interesting to see how programmes are put together. The individual pieces that they film are called 'rushes', which are all carefully documented so that they can be found again for editing purposes. The details of the rushes are written on to 'Post-it' stickers, and these are arranged on the wall into groups for including in different programmes. A sticker can get moved about a lot, or even removed, depending on the results of recent filming and what the director thinks will work best.

I had a job coming up that I thought Rupert might be interested in, but felt it would be useful for him to look at it first before deciding whether to film there or not.

We all drove over to Waltham Abbey, to a friend whom I have known for several years through the local Hardy Plant Society. It was about three years ago that Mavis Riley asked me to help clear her overgrown garden and replant it for her. After that, sadly, her husband became ill and subsequently died, and she has been unwell herself, so looking after the garden was postponed for some time and it has got into rather a mess.

Rupert agreed that the job might make interesting filming, so we arranged with Mavis a couple of dates when we could call and carry out the work, hoping to start in a week's time.

I got back home, before driving on to a horticultural society near Newbury to give them my new talk on 'The Making of *Christine's Garden*'. This society is quite a small one, but they had opened the meeting to other societies, and altogether there were about 100 people in the audience.

They seemed to be interested in what I told them about the process of making the series, all the equipment that has to be brought into my garden and the ups and downs that occur, both in the process of filming and simply through having another three people in my home.

*

19 July
This was a welcome day spent at home catching up with lots of domestic and work-related jobs.

I have never enjoyed the sun, and am struggling to cope with the heat, spending some time just lying on the bed, as I feel so done in. I find this very frustrating as I have much to do, but cannot motivate myself. I am longing for a thunderstorm, rain and the resulting coolness.

*

20–21 July
I went back up to the Kirklees Light Railway for a couple of days, to discuss the way forward. With all projects, when new people take over, there are teething problems.

We are having difficulties recruiting volunteers for the planting that needs to be completed and continuing maintenance. We don't have a database of information, and are trying to do too many jobs at once.

We got together all the staff who are involved

with the projects I am overseeing, and had a site visit to see what could be achieved. This was useful, as it meant they heard it from the horse's mouth, as it were!

It was decided that next year would be a time of consolidation. New developments would be put on hold to give everyone involved time to get to know each other, and to complete existing work on the site.

During this visit I had hoped to plant up 24 hanging baskets and two large containers, with the help of volunteers. Unfortunately, this had not been organized, so I went with Michael, the newly appointed gardener, to the local garden centre to see what planting material was available there.

We walked around and put a planting list together for the hanging baskets, which included *Campanula carpatica* 'Blue Clips' and 'White Clips', non-stop begonias, New Guinea impatiens, mixed thymus cultivars and some different variegated ivy plants. It is a difficult time of the year to be making up baskets, as the bedding plant season is over, and the range of other suitable material is rather limited.

We then decided we would make up the two large containers on site with shrubs, as they would give all-year-round interest. We decided to use *Leucothoe* 'Zeblid', *Euonymus fortunei* 'Emerald Gaiety' and some golden forms of *Erica carnea*. We would need to use some ericaceous compost for these two tubs, as most of the plants we selected prefer acid conditions.

There wasn't time on this visit for me to oversee the planting, so, having chosen the plants, I asked Michael to speak to the volunteers and organize a planting day with them.

*

22–24 July
These were still very hot days and I resorted to the continental way of working early and late, with a siesta in between. Watering the garden is taking a considerable amount of time at present.

One evening was spent socializing with my neighbours. I had popped round for just a quick drink but, as so often occurs on these occasions, we all relaxed and, before we knew it, Pat was in the kitchen making prawn and salmon wraps and Louse was in her kitchen making steak and chips for us all. Needless to say, I stayed much longer then I had anticipated.

*

25 July
Rupert and the crew turned up at 7 a.m., as they wanted to see me watering the garden using my bath-water. For some strange reason they thought this very eccentric. I explained to them that, when facing a drought, gardeners up and down the country will do all they can to keep their plants alive.

Using soapy water on plants is not a problem, as long as you do not do it permanently. If you did, in the long term the salts in the soapy bathwater—or the detergent contained in washing-up water— could cause problems to root growth.

I bail the water out of the bath using buckets, and then carry these outside. I have tried using the siphoning method, but I am not always successful, as it really is a two-person job.

While Rupert was getting shots of the front garden, Sarah noticed a grey furry cat sitting on my fence. I had noticed something there, but did not see it was a cat. As we got nearer, Sarah started laughing and I asked her what it was she was laughing at. She said that what she thought was a grey furry cat was really the grey cover to Jimmy's boom microphone. I must admit that I hadn't seen it move in some time!

When we'd finished and I was due to leave to drive to my friend Mavis Riley's house, Rupert asked me to say to camera where I was going. I said, 'To a friend's to do some gardening.' He and Sarah kept asking me to repeat this to get it sounding right. Sometimes I really do not have the foggiest idea what they are expecting me to say or the manner in which they would like it said. No doubt they know what they want in their own minds, but they don't seem to be able to explain it to me, and when I do not say it in the way they expect, it causes disappointment. Rupert kept trying to get the answer he wanted, but in the end I got the impression that the reply I gave still wasn't right!

I arrived at Mavis's home in Waltham Cross. The gardens, both front and back, are not very big but have become overgrown since Mavis's husband's death. Mavis looked after Walter at home while she could cope, and afterwards she was not well herself. Mavis had spoken to me about going over earlier in the year, but I was just too busy and today was the first date that was convenient for us both.

When I saw the garden, it was bad but not as bad as it had been the very first time I cleared and replanted it. The front garden was very overgrown with a potato vine (*Solanum crispum* 'Glasnevin'), *Ceratostigma willmottianum*, *Pyracantha coccinea*, plus various geraniums, euphorbias and all sorts of things that had dried up in the drought.

Mavis explained that, in the past, the potato vine had been trained along the wall of the house, but I could see no stem on that side of the garden, so I cut it back vigorously. Perhaps I will find the main stem at some point and be able to train it back against the wall.

*

26 July

Rupert wanted to show me doing the various odd jobs that needed completing in my garden today, and he started by filming me dead-heading the summer bedding plants. At one stage he asked me how I thought the garden was looking, and my reply was 'OK'. He did not seem very happy with this, and he said it was the first time he had ever heard me play down my garden.

I explained that the light was flat, and the garden was doing nothing for me at all, in the heat, at this time of day—after all, it was 28°C (82°F). He kept asking me the same question, presumably to encourage a better answer. In the end, because I was not giving him what he wanted, we decided to have a break. I went on to explain that the garden did do things for me in the early morning and in the evenings as the temperature got cooler, but I hate this time of the year. When it's *so* hot the plants really suffer and I just do not enjoy the garden so much.

On occasions I really do struggle to understand

what Rupert is looking for. He will have something in his head, but doesn't seem to know exactly what until he actually hears it from me. Sometimes, the way we film can be very frustrating for us all, I suspect, but this morning I felt I could not produce a single thing he wanted. I am not sure if it was the heat, but I was not enjoying it, and was getting more and more annoyed with myself.

After lunch we went into the Essex countryside to get some shots of me driving along country lanes. These shots are used to link various bits of film together. While we were out it started to thunder and, for the first time in ages, we had some rain. Rupert decided that we should return quickly to the garden and take advantage of it.

Unfortunately, the rain did not last that long, but he did catch me running about the garden in the rain. I wanted it to rain for hours and hours, not just half an hour. However, it was enough to make the garden perk up, the colours were looking great and he did manage to get some nice bits of film from me—at least, he seemed much happier than he did during the frustrating morning.

All in all, I found today one of the most difficult days of filming I've known. Because of the heat, I am still not sleeping very well and I am very tired. I'm happy if the temperature is in the seventies, but not in the eighties and above. Today I really struggled with it all and, for the first time, was not enjoying what I was doing. I did apologize to Rupert later in the day, and he told me not to worry, as some days are just like that. Perhaps I will feel better when it's cooler. I hope so!

✳

27 July

A chap I did some work for many years ago rang me again recently to ask if I could go over to his new home and have a look at his yew hedge (*Taxus baccata*), which was dying. I commented then that I was impressed that he remembered me, as it was probably 14 years since I had done any work for him. He said that his wife always retained the details of people who they felt had done a good job. She had found my card and they hoped I would be in a position to help them once again.

I found when I arrived that the yews were 1.5m (5 feet) high and had been planted, in February, into a heavy clay soil. Some of them were growing, while others were brown and dried out, having failed to produce any new root growth at all.

I was told that the supplier had been to the site and had said that the site was too wet, and it was this that had killed the problem trees. I decided to remove one of them and to dig a deep hole to see what the soil was like at depth. I was looking for either red flecking or a grey colour which would indicate a high or fluctuating water table, respectively. As it turned out I found no indication of any drainage problem, and nothing to indicate that the soil had been wet for any period of time.

On further examination, looking at the rootball, I came to the conclusion that the trees that had died had probably dried out prior to the supplier even getting them. I explained this to my client and his gardener, who were going to speak to the supplier again. If necessary I might be called in to deliver my opinion first hand.

I find this investigative aspect of my work really fascinating, as I have to draw on all my knowledge, and experience in all aspects of horticulture, to come to a conclusion.

In the evening I drove over to Kirby to give a talk to the gardening club there, this time on 'Hardy plants for the garden'. I am always made very welcome at this club. A lot of the members listen to me regularly on BBC Essex, and because of this they understand that I need to eat food at regular intervals. I broadcast live from 12 noon to 2 p.m. and find that, even if I eat just before I drive over to Chelmsford, it is too long a gap before I get home without eating again, so I take a packed lunch with me. The presenter of the programme often teases me, on air, for eating my lunch during the one o'clock news, so people have become aware of my habit.

At Kirby they are so thoughtful that they bring me a lovely hamper of sandwiches, salad and a pudding, plus something to drink. They know that I leave my house at 5.30 p.m and will not be back home until after 11 p.m., so they give me the opportunity to eat something before I leave them. Now that is the way to ensure that a speaker will return! I also find it very touching that someone has thought about me, and has gone to all this effort.

*

28 July
I spent the entire day working in the office preparing course material for next term at Writtle College, which starts in September, answering the phone about work-related matters and writing.

*

I had recently been invited to a vineyard by a young chap who had attended one of my courses on maximizing sales within farm shops and farmers' markets. His vineyard Shawgate is up in Suffolk, so it was a reasonable drive and it gave me the opportunity to see the effect of the long drought on the countryside.

I was seeing burnt-up grass verges, trees that were losing their leaves and looking very thin in the canopy, wheat that was ripening and being harvested and a very dry, hot, tired landscape. We could do with a substantial amount of rain in this part of the world at the moment.

The visit involved a tour of the vineyard, which grows seven different grape varieties and, most unusually for an English vineyard, two red varieties, namely 'Rondo' and 'Acolon'.

One of the things that I found interesting was their method of pruning. Many amateurs, when pruning grapes, will remove a lot of the leaves to ensure that the sun gets to the grapes as they ripen. At this vineyard they try to retain at least 15 leaves per bunch of grapes, and also have the rows running north to south to maximize the light reaching the bunches on both sides of the rows.

Before lunch we had a wine-tasting session. Who said that the English can't make excellent wine? I would challenge anyone to try wine from this vineyard and not be delighted with it. We tried five different whites, ranging from dry to a dessert wine. They were all very drinkable and a couple of them were very nice indeed.

My social activities continued on the Sunday, when I went to see have lunch with a past student.

She is a garden designer, and I was keen to see how her garden was developing. It was planted up with reduced water availability in mind and also with the knowledge that in time gardening will become difficult because of her arthritis.

The garden was looking stunning. It has a very tropical feel, with tree ferns, bananas, cannas, Chusan palm, Canary Island date palm, the Mexican blue palm and the Californian cotton palm, plus lots of cacti and succulents, begonias and salvias. These were set off with some lovely pots and urns surrounding a pond containing one water lily and a lot of fish and frogs. It was lovely, and you would find it hard to believe, when sitting in the garden, that you were in Essex, and not Italy or the south of France.

*

31 July
I spent the whole day cutting my hedges, in both the front and back gardens, with a mechanical hedge trimmer.

All the clippings were mixed with other vegetation and then put in my compost bins.

I cannot stress enough that mixing the clippings with other material breaks them down far quicker than just putting them in the bin in layers.

AUGUST

1 August
Over the past ten years I've been maintaining a garden in Epping Forest. This is the garden and house that Brigid has been looking after since two of our mutual friends died. Today I drove over there, probably for the final time. I feel sad about this as I enjoyed gardening there and the couple were so nice.

I spent most of the day weeding beds and paths by hand and then cleaning out the greenhouse so that the place looked tidy. I feel sad that an era has come to an end. I knew the people very well, and all those lovely times will now be just memories.

*

2 August
A professional photographer came for most of the day, and worked with me in my garden, taking shots for this book.

This event was much easier than normal as I already knew the photographer and we did not have to get to know each other beforehand. I find it helps a lot if you feel happy with the personality of the person who is trying to capture your image. We did some shots in the vegetable garden and the rest in the main part of the garden.

What was interesting was that he was shooting both on film and with a digital camera, so he could actually show me at once what he had taken, and he was keen to let me see what he was framing in his viewfinder. He also asked me for suggestions which I appreciated.

✱

3 August

Rupert and the gang were with me today, filming a visit to a local garden centre to select plants for Louise's border.

She has seven fencing panels, which need to be covered with plants, plus a border that is approximately 1–1.2m (3–4 feet) wide and 12m (40 feet) long. Louise is still in the early stages of learning about gardening, so she had no idea what to buy. When asked what she fancied, she was very honest and said she simply did not know.

I suggested that the best thing to do was to look at the plants and select things she liked, and I would then comment on their suitability.

We had already carried out a soil pH test, so we knew that it was neutral. This means we can select a very wide range of plants, but would be wise to avoid acid-lovers.

We started with the problem of the fencing panels. As a rough guide, one plant per panel, with each panel being approximately 2m (6 feet) in length, is a good start—although some plants can cover several panels very quickly. In the end we selected six plants.

Abutilon 'Kentish Belle' may need protecting in winter with a fleece covering, but I have one in my garden that is fine. Louise's border faces south and is hot, so I am optimistic that it will be OK.

Clematis montana, new to me, 'Miss Christine' was chosen for its name. The information on the label showed it was a recent introduction. The white flower with a pink back sounded very nice,

211

and I decided I would get one for myself. It would be nice to have a plant with my name in the garden, and I am, after all, a 'Miss Christine'.

Louise selected another clematis, *Clematis* 'Galore', and, for their scent, she picked *Jasminum polyanthum*, *Solanum crispum* and *Campsis radicans*.

We then concentrated on the border, and I suggested that she got some plants that would come up every year, so we headed off for the herbaceous perennial section. She selected *Anemone* 'Königin Charlotte', *Rudbeckia fulgida* var. *sullivantii* 'Goldsturm', *Festuca glauca* 'Azurit', *Chrysanthemum* 'Silver Princess', *Penstemon* 'Rich Ruby', *Crocosmia* x *crocosmiiflora* 'Babylon', *Artemisia schmidtiana*, *Aster* 'Tonga' and *Helenium* 'Coppelia'. We added a few shrubs including *Euonymus japonicus* 'Aureopictus', *Lavendula* 'Hidcote' and *Coronilla valentina* 'Variegata'.

By the time we got home I had to leave Louise, as I had an evening appointment. I advised her to keep her plants in the shade and water them well until I could show her how to position and plant them.

I also asked her to obtain six large bags of good-quality compost and to dig this into the border, in preparation for planting. The compost would help retain moisture in the soil, as Louise's soil is like mine, very light and well-drained. It needs additional organic matter to act like a sponge and hold on to water; otherwise it just drains straight through.

*

4 August

Rupert was still keen to see me siphoning my bath-water out into the garden instead of using buckets. I've been trying this again and having a bit more success. It sounds easy, but I have to lift the water in the hose-pipe 6 feet up from the bath and through the window before it starts the downwards journey, and that takes a lot of hard sucking on the end of the hose to get it going.

My early attempts did not work, so I reduced the length of the pipe and, eventually, after a lot of effort, got the water to flow. As a method, it is somewhat easier than carrying the water down the stairs in buckets. My mail order pump still hasn't arrived.

I then went round to see if Reg was at home. I have been promising to reduce the height of his *Magnolia* x *soulangeana*. The shrub is about 4.2m (14 feet) tall and is taking away all the light from his patio. It is such a height that Reg has to use a ladder when he prunes it and, to be honest, I do not think it is really safe for him to do that these days.

My intention was to reduce it to about 2.4m (8 feet). This involved, first, removing all the growth to about 3m (10 feet) so I could see what I was doing. I then identified dormant buds around old scars on the stem and I pruned down to this level. New growth will shoot from these regions. The shrub may not flower that well this coming spring, but it does mean that now Reg can attend to it without going up a ladder.

*

5–7 August

I spent some time visiting friends and writing. I then drove over to Buckhurst Hill to carry out a gardening job at the flats where I recently cut the hedge. Today's task was to fork out all the cornflowers, asters and pot marigolds from the rose borders, which were looking very untidy. The borders had not been weeded for some time.

From past experience the asters are likely to reappear where the roots have grown under the rose bushes, and then I cannot get them out without damaging the roots of the roses, and the seeds of the marigolds remain in the soil to come up again next year.

I am also hopeful that with so much growth having been removed from among the rose bushes, air circulation will improve and mildew and black spot may not be as bad as they have been in the past.

When I returned home Tara was not around, so I went over to Reg's. Reg, Pat and Louise were on the patio and Tara was sunning herself with them. I joined them for a glass of wine and some nibbles. Louise and I talked about our working day, and Reg described his day—sitting in the sun on the patio! It's all right for some.

✳

8 August

I went to help Brigid pack books and other items as the house in Epping Forest that she has been living for the past three years has been sold, and the new owners move in soon. We both felt sad, but we will have lovely memories of her time there, and of the couple who owned the house and the garden that I have looked after for some time.

I think moving is an awful experience, especially if you have lived in your home some time and been happy there. You casually pick up some item and find that it triggers memories of events in the past. Moving on is difficult, even if you know it's the right thing to do.

As I pulled out of the driveway for the last time, I had tears in my eyes. I suppose, in many ways, this is a tribute to the people I knew who had died. They both had so much sensitivity and compassion to share with everyone they met. I do not believe I shall ever meet such a couple again, and the world is a poorer place without them.

9 August

I returned to Mavis Riley's home in Waltham Cross to finish clearing the front garden.

Eventually I was sucessful in finding the main stem of the solanum (the potato vine) that Mavis would like me to train back along the wall of the house and under her window. However, to do this I have had to completely remove the pyracantha that had grown through the solanum and was preventing me training it against the wall.

This was a very dry, dusty job which, once again, Rupert and the film crew came to shoot. It is not an ideal setting in which to film, as the road on which Mavis lives has a horrendous amount of traffic. Rupert would ask me a question and, as soon as I started to reply, Jimmy would tell me to stop because of the noise. This situation, over the day, tried all our patience. If it was not cars, lorries or planes, it was tin cans blowing down the road, noisy wheelchairs, motorbikes, or people stopping in cars and asking us what we were filming!

When there are frequent interruptions I find it even more difficult to concentrate on Rupert's questions, and it seems to happen invariably when Rupert wants some emotional comment from me. The line of questioning is then abandoned until we are somewhere less noisy. I look forward to getting into Mavis's back garden, where there should be much less disruption.

By the end of the day I had cleared the garden sufficiently to allow me, on my next visit, to train in the solanum and prepare the soil for planting.

On the way home we passed through some lovely open countryside over which a combine harvester was harvesting the wheat. The sun was setting and it looked very beautiful. I was driving in front of the crew's car when I noticed its lights were flashing. Instantly, I had an idea what Rupert was thinking, and I was right.

Once we had both parked, he came over and said he would like to get a 'drive through' along the road with the lovely sun setting behind the car. The request did not surprise me. This took about another hour. Once Rupert had got his shots we then set off home again.

✱

10 August
The crew turned up for another day's filming, this time partly in my garden, but also with Reg in his garden and Louise in hers.

The three of us are having a light-hearted competition to see whose tomatoes are the best, and we have decided that it would be fun if we

216

entered them into a flower show to let someone else judge them, independently. In practice none of us expects to win a thing because we have not used show varieties, and have not given any of our plants the attention to detail required to grow winning produce. However, it should be fun.

Rupert wanted my comments on what I was looking for in my vegetable garden, when selecting items for showing.

Any produce selected should be healthy, with few or no blemishes, typical of the item you are showing, the correct size as detailed in the show schedule and a good shape, and that, if you are showing several of the same thing, they should look as similar as possible.

I may have tomatoes, courgettes, carrots, potatoes and onions to enter, but, as is normal when showing, the timing is essential, it will depend on what is right just before the show takes place.

I then went round to see what the competition was like at Reg's and Louise's. Reg should have tomatoes, shallots, onions and possibly carrots to enter, while Louise may have tomatoes. Reg and Louise have the normal-sized tomatoes while mine are the cherry type, so I may already be at a disadvantage, due the difference in size, but time will tell.

In the afternoon I worked with Louise, planting up her border with the plants we had bought last week. We had some great fun positioning the plants, as although Louise was aware of the basic rule that tall plants should mainly be towards the back, while shorter ones come forward, she had no idea of what should go next to what.

I said it would be best to put the climbers in first, and positioned these against the fence. In placing them I took into consideration their rate of growth, when they bloom, what colour flowers they have, and how they will look against each other and the plants we will be planting in front of them.

Before planting the climbers we dug large holes, which will allow space to spread out the roots, and then filled the holes with water. In dry weather this helps the plants to establish, ensuring that water gets down below the roots, which it doesn't always do when applied to the surface of the soil.

Something Louise had not thought about was how these plants were going to be supported, given that the fencing panels she wished to cover were not hers.

One of the easiest methods is to put in fencing posts, in front of the existing fence, 6 feet apart. You then drill holes in them all the way up about a foot apart, and thread strong wire through the holes. This wire will support the foliage, keep it off the fencing panels and also allow air to circulate behind the plants and so help to reduce diseases such as mildew.

We then moved on to planting the herbaceous perennial plants, which will come up every year, and the shrubs. We arranged these so that the taller plants were distributed throughout the border rather than having all the tall plants at the back, the medium-sized ones in the middle and the small ones at the front. That gives a stepped effect, which is undesirable. It's best not to be able to see every plant straight way when you look along the border. Hiding some of them behind others creates a sense of mystery and discovery as you move along.

Once we got everything planted, we then spent about an hour watering these in. It is important that you water plants in well to ensure no air pockets remain around the root system or the roots will not grow outwards. If you apply a little water and allow it to soak in it before adding more, it won't all just run off the surface. I asked Louse to start at one end of the border and then, when she got to the other end, to start all over again.

We then stood back and agreed that it did look nice. After we'd put the tools away and cleaned up, Reg, Pat and Colin joined us for a drink, and we sat in the garden chatting about the plants and colour that, all being well, Louise and Colin will enjoy in the years to come.

*

11–14 August
Between stints of writing I went into the garden for a change of activity. During these breaks I did some dead-heading and started taking cuttings of plants which are too tender to over-winter outside.

I like to take them now as there is sufficient light to enable them to grow and produce roots before the days shorten. My experience has shown that the later I take them, in August and September, the more losses I have.

The plants I take cuttings from include coleus, now called solenostemon, diascia, salvia, fuchsia, pelargonium, heliotropium, helichrysum, plectranthus, argyranthemum and verbena.

I find that having a few cuttings in a pot takes up far less space than trying to accommodate all the parent plants, which are quite large. Once these cuttings start into growth again in the spring, I then take cuttings from them and bulk up my numbers in this way.

> *The method I use is to take about 8cm (3 inches) of the growing tips of shoots, cut from the parent plant just under a leaf joint, then remove the lower leaves to two or three pairs and push the cuttings into pots full of multipurpose compost, and water.*

The pots are placed on the kitchen windowsill and kept well watered. If the cuttings wilt, I will put a plastic bag upside down over the pot and cuttings to retain moisture, until they have rooted and are capable of taking up water for themselves.

I have picked my first sweet corn! I so look forward to this. It is one of the best crops to take straight off the plant, cook and eat. I always boil it for about ten minutes in salted water, then drain it, melt butter in the saucepan and pour this along with lemon juice over the cobs. Add lots of black pepper and you have a feast!

✳

5–17 August
I went to Abercarn, in South Wales, to give some advice on a friend's garden, which was beginning to get overgrown. The state of this garden is the result

a very common mistake: planting too many plants in the first place.

Even when given the right amount of space, when the plants start to grow, and fill their allotted area, they should be thinned out to give more space to the choice plants, the ones that you wish to retain. If not, the effect is overcrowding—plants grow into and spoil each other.

In practice it is better to start by putting into the garden those plants you want as permanent features, and then fill in the surplus space with temporary plants, such as annuals or bedding plants, until the permanent plants have attained their height and spread. Very few people will remove trees or shrubs, even if they have used these as temporary fillers, and this is where things go wrong.

Yvonne and I walked round the garden, and I suggested various plants that needed pruning and some which should be removed altogether. Because Yvonne does not have a lot of spare time, I also suggested that in the resulting spaces she then put down a heavy-duty landscape fabric and cover it with at least 8cm (3 inches) of bark mulch, as this would considerably reduce the amount of work necessary to keep the garden looking tidy.

I thought that she would be better off getting someone in to do all this work for her. That was when the fun started. She didn't know anyone in the area who did this type of work and didn't know how to find anyone.

We looked at Yellow Pages and the web. I advised that the best people to consider were those belonging to professional organizations such as the Association of Professional Landscapers (APL), the Horticultural Trades Association (HTA), the Garden Centre Association (GCA), the British Association of Landscape Industries (BALI) or the Society of Garden Designers (SGD), as their members have to work to official standards and codes of conduct.

We tried phoning several people and left messages, but they did not reply.

One chap who turned up was as uninspiring as I have ever seen. He was dull, did not explain what he thought he might do, took very few measurements, did not question Yvonne on what she wanted, did not ask when she wanted the work to be completed by, could not fully identify mint when it was in flower and just said he would put some ideas in the post. Before he even got off the premises Yvonne was saying she did not take to him. This was hardly surprising.

Some of what he said was technically correct, but his dull manner left a lot to be desired. It would be fascinating to see what he puts in the post, if indeed he does. Yvonne tried a garden centre which was going to send someone out, but I had to leave before they arrived.

This activity did highlight a common problem facing people trying to find someone suitable to carry out work. Where do you begin? How do you know what help to ask for if you do not know anything about the subject, or know anyone who could help?

*

18–21 August
This weekend was spent completely outdoors, camping in the New Forest with my friend Penny.

She wanted to give her puppy, Indie, the new experience of camping, and we thought it would be nice if I went along as well with Tara, so she could show the puppy a thing or two.

We had a lovely visit and the first day spent our time walking the dogs and enjoying the wild flowers, which were looking lovely. Just outside the campsite we saw the attractive scarlet pimpernel (*Anagallis arvensis*) and common centaury (*Centaurium erythraea*), with its glossy leaves and pretty pink petals, picked up the fragrance, and then saw, wild thyme (*Thymus praecox* subsp. *articus*), noticed the just-opening flower buds of red clover (*Trifolium pratense*) and also, growing almost through it, the hop trefoil (*Trifolium campestre*). What was interesting was the fact that this area was covered in mainly native flowers. I could not help wondering if this was due to the grazing pressure of the ponies, restricting the survival of those wild flowers introduced by birds.

The next day we decided to go to the coast at Lepe, and visit the country park. This is a stretch of land adjoining the Solent, and lying within an area of outstanding natural beauty.

Penny and I both expected Indie to go straight into the sea, but to our amusement it was Tara, who has never been one for water but must have felt it was up to her to show Indie what to do, that rushed in. I did not even have a towel with me, as she normally never goes near water. Indie showed no interest whatsoever in going in but I think Tara may have been thinking, 'I'm getting on so I'm going to do all those things I haven't done yet.' Old age is such a funny thing!

Along the coast, the flora in the sand dunes,

which mainly had been planted, looked very much like the New Zealand coast, in places, with cordylines and phormiums growing through pampas grass (*Cortaderia selloana*). The smaller, wild flowers included the curious, succulent-leaved member of the carrot family, the rock samphire (*Crithmum maritimum*) growing on the rocks.

*

23 August

Back home again, and I removed a *Jasminum beesianum* from the west side of my shed and planted a *Clematis montana* 'Miss Christine' in its place. Before planting the clematis I dug a large hole for the root system, filled the hole with water and placed some slow-release fertilizer capsules into the bottom of the hole. I planted the root system about 8cm (3 inches) below the soil surface, as this helps in the event of clematis wilt. If I find the plant does suffer from this, I will prune it right down to the ground, and then, normally, it will produce new shoots from dormant buds on the stem below the ground.

My alpine sinks have been looking tired lately, so I removed some of the very old plants, and those which had got too large for their positions, and replant the sinks with a selection of plants. These included *Hypericum aegypticum*, *H. polyphyllum* 'Grandiflorum', *Silene acaulis* subsp. *acaulis*, *Phlox subulata* 'Marjorie', *Penstemon pinifolius*, *Papaver miyabeanum* and a dwarf form of *Iris setosa*.

I replaced some of the old soil from the sinks with a mixture of equal parts John Innes potting compost No. 2 and sharp grit. After planting, I then re-dressed the top of the sinks with a sharp gravel and watered the plants in.

After harvesting a large quantity of tomatoes I decided to use some to make tomato soup. I never measure anything when I make soup. All I do is put about 2.5cm (1 inch) of vegetable stock in a saucepan; chop up and add the tomatoes until they fill the saucepan to within 5cm (2 inches) of the top of the pan; chop up two large onions and put those in the saucepan with the tomatoes; add salt and black pepper; bring to the boil, and then simmer it all for 30 minutes, before liquidizing and serving.

I made a very large amount of this soup today, as I wanted to put some into the freezer, to be eaten on cold winter's evenings. I will sometimes have this soup along with Welsh rarebit.

*

24–25 August
Rupert spent these two days filming Reg and me getting vegetables ready for the horticultural show we are attending on Monday where we will find out who has the best tomatoes. I still suspect Reg will do better than me, as his are bigger and are grown in a greenhouse.

While we both have tomatoes and carrots to show, Reg is also putting in three onions and nine shallots. He has never shown before, so he came round to ask me how to get his onions and shallots prepared for the show.

The preparation involves removing the dry, outer skins without revealing the white leaves underneath, trimming off the roots against the basal plate and tying the tops neatly with raffia or thread. This tying proved very entertaining, as Reg has got very big hands and just could not manage to tie a neat knot to finish off the job. I had to do this for him.

*

26–27 August

I was over at college carrying out a weekend course on basic garden design. We looked at initial site analysis, which covers aspects such as orientation, where are the services are, the topography of the land, any views from the garden, and whether they are worth keeping, the boundaries, the type and style of dwellings, access to the site and people's requirements from the garden. You note the state of repair of all features. What plants, trees and shrubs are already there? What is the soil like—drainage, pH—and are there any indicator weeds present? What is the climate like? Does the garden experience frost pockets? How much time is available to look after the garden? What are the planning and legal constraints?

Time is then spent on the principles of garden design such as topography, unity, balance, proportion and scale, variety, simplicity, seasonality, time, costs, colour. I generally take the students outside to look around the college grounds and point out all these features, or set them exercises to help them understand what I have been explaining in the classroom.

We then all have a go at chain surveying. This is the point at which most people begin to get an idea why professionals charge a fee for this aspect of garden design. It is time-consuming as it does have to be really accurate.

Once the students have all noted down sufficient measurements and are happy with what they have recorded, we then go into the drawing studios to transfer their information to paper.

This is always fun to watch. At first the students often don't seem to believe that, even having carefully taken down the information, they will ever produce a proper plan of what they measured, but in the course of the afternoon they all eventually get the hang of it. Once again, this work underlines the skill and time a professional garden designer brings to the job.

For me the best bit of this weekend course is looking at the soft landscaping—the plants. We go outside and walk around the grounds, and I point out plants and draw attention to differences in habits, height, use, colour, seasonality and so on. Much time is spent just chatting about the plants and how they grow and the ways they can be used.

I conclude the weekend by looking at hard landscaping—the bricks, gravels, fences, buildings, paths and such items as seating which bring the whole design together.

The students always comment that, prior to the course, they had very little idea of what design really involved and what skills were necessary to pull it off well. I enjoy teaching this course very much, as I can tell that the students are thinking all the time and really get a lot out of the two days they spend at the college.

I returned home and washed all the carrots that I was taking to the show, and then prepared all the vegetables, both mine and Reg's, for transporting in the car, as we need to leave early in the morning to get to the show. Pat has also decided to enter, and has made one of her fantastic fruit pies. I told her that I bet she wins a prize.

*

28 August

Reg, Pat and I left the house early to drive over to Brightlingsea, where the show was being held. I chose this particular flower show for us to enter because I am known to the members of the gardening club there through my lectures, and one of these lectures was filmed for *Christine's Garden* last year. Rupert and the crew joined us to film the show.

I had taken along some silver sand so that Reg could stage his shallots on a plate of it; we had made rings of it so that his onions could sit on the bench properly, and I had taken some carrot foliage to act as a background to our tomatoes, which are normally just displayed on a paper plate. The carrots are just laid on the bench. Pat's pie looked excellent, almost too tempting to leave unattended!

Once we had staged our produce, the three of us went off to get some breakfast while the judging was taking place. I knew I did not have a chance in the tomato class, as most of the entries were glasshouse grown like Reg's, but I was hopeful that Reg might get something, as his were a very nice size and shape and evenly coloured. His onions also stood a chance, in my opinion, but our carrots were on the small side. Pat's pie looked great on the show bench.

We went down the sea front to the prom, found a café and had a great fried breakfast that set us up

228

for the day. The cafe is in a lovely position, as while you are eating you can see all the well-maintained and differently coloured beach huts and, out on the water, the smacks and barges that Brightlingsea is famous for.

While sitting eating our breakfast, a lot of people came over, having recognized the three of us from the series, and made some nice comments about it. This amused Reg very much, and he kept saying that I was famous! I have to keep reminding him that he and Pat are now asked about wherever I go, and they too are widely recognized.

When we returned to the hall the judging was still going on, so we walked around the stalls where people were selling cakes, beer and plants, and watched the local dog show. This was fun, as it even had a class for the waggiest tail. I wished I had brought Tara.

At midday the hall was opened and all exhibitors rushed in to see how they had done. As I thought, our carrots were not placed, but Reg had got a third in the onion class and was thrilled with this. He kept saying it was due to my tuition in show preparation. He also got third place for his tomatoes, which pleased me enormously. He was so excited as my little 'Sungolds' didn't get anything! So that decided it—Reg was the better of the two of us at growing tomatoes. He was the Tomato King.

It was all the more enjoyable for Reg as he had never shown before, but he did comment that he thought it was unfair to have outdoor grown tomatoes, like mine, being judged against glasshouse grown ones. I do not think he said this just to make me feel better. It was just typical of his generous, fair-minded nature.

Off we went to see how Pat had got on, and I was the first to see that she had got a prize card. I couldn't see at first what she had got, but encouraged her to come and look. In the car, during our journey this morning, she said that she did not have a chance of getting a prize, as she does not even use a recipe to make her pies. I had other thoughts. I do not usually like apple pie, and will never order it if I am eating out; but I would kill for one of Pat's pies. They are fantastic. The pastry melts in your mouth and the fruit has just a hint of tartness—absolutely great.

As we all got near enough to see, Pat gasped when she saw she had got first prize but I wasn't surprised at all. Pat has never made me a single pie, over the 15 years that I have known her, which has not been delicious. So, there I was with two 77-year-olds, who have never shown anything in their lives before, both with prizes. It was a wonderful moment for all of us.

When we got home we celebrated by eating the pie and enjoying a bottle of wine together. It was lovely to see the two of them with their prize cards. Reg said he would have to get them framed.

*

28–31 August
I went to stay with my friends Carole and Stephen in Witney, just relaxing and enjoying each other's company. They took me to see Kingston Bagpuize, a lovely house, with an interesting garden, that I had not visited before.

I am not normally a great fan of conducted tours, but the mother of the present owner took a small group of visitors around the house, and explained the main items of interest in a caring and loving manner without being too sentimental. Only one comment from her gave away that it was a family member who was conducting the tour, otherwise you would not have known.

The baroque house sits happily in a small park surrounded by some fascinating plantings of beautiful and unusual trees and shrubs. Within the parkland is a garden which, even for an experienced and well-travelled plantsperson, is well worth seeing because of its unusual trees and shrubs. The very deep herbaceous border must be a challenge to maintain without constant forking over every time you walk on the bed.

We also spent some time in a second-hand bookshop. Carol knows my love of books, and also the subjects that I am interested in, and this one had an excellent selection on bell-ringing.

I used to ring regularly, but as a freelance I now have very irregular work patterns, so I can't commit myself to a tower. I do not believe this is an activity to get involved with unless you are always available to ring on Sundays and at other services when needed.

SEPTEMBER

1–3 September

I spent some time preparing a talk I was going to give, over the weekend, at the King's Heath Park Flower Show in Birmingham. I had been asked to give two presentations about the making of *Christine's Garden*, and also to join other experts on a gardeners' question time panel, which would take place six times over the weekend.

I drove up to a friend's house which is only a few minutes away from the park. It was lovely of Doreen to ask me and Tara to stay with her, and it also made the whole weekend so much easier and more relaxing than having to stay in yet another hotel.

People often say it must be lovely staying in hotels all around the country. Well, if you speak to anyone who does this a lot, the answer you usually get is that they end up eating food that they don't really fancy, trying to get to sleep in a bed that is not like their own, finding they can't open the window, so they die of heat, or they turn on the air-conditioning and then freeze all night, or else find the noise so irritating that it keeps them awake. Do not get me wrong, some hotels are very nice, but a lot are just somewhere to put your head until the morning.

The show itself was great. Lots of tents with the specialist societies inside. The National Begonia Society had a fantastic display, not only of flowering types, but also of ones grown for their foliage. The vegetables, fuchsias and many other flowers all reflected the love and care given to make them so beautiful on the day.

Lots of nurseries were there with great bargains. I was surprised at the excellent value that was being offered at very reasonable prices. A French market provided me with the opportunity to try all sorts of delicious food and drink. I love places where I can try things. Being on my own, I do not always want to buy a family-sized item if I am not sure I am going to like it.

The weather on the Saturday was wet and chilly, but it did not keep people away. The Sunday was a glorious day, filled with sunshine, and the place was heaving with keen gardeners all out to enjoy themselves. All the sessions I did were well supported, with people keen to hear how a television series is made.

The gardeners' question time threw up a few interesting issues such as the problem of pear rust. This is fairly rare in Britain, and I have only ever seen it once before. It is an interesting disease as it spends the winter, as spores, on junipers. It shows itself, in the spring and summer, as red spots on the surface of pear leaves which darken as the season progresses. The only remedy is to clear up all the fallen leaves in the autumn and, if you have a juniper in the garden, it may be worth removing it so that the disease cannot over-winter. There is no chemical treatment available for it.

*

4 September
I spent the morning in the garden taking softwood cuttings from lamiums, fuchsias, geraniums, euryops and oxalis. I like to take them at this time

of the year so that the roots will form, and the plants will be a reasonable size, as we go into the winter. These are all put into 8-cm (3-inch) plastic pots containing multipurpose compost. I usually put three or four cuttings into each pot, water them well and then put them on the kitchen windowsill.

I also spent time cutting back the foliage of hellebores almost to ground level, so that I could see the freshly emerging flowers of *Cyclamen hederifolium* underneath them. I just love this time of the year when all my cyclamen start to bloom. These little shuttlecock-like flowers give me so much pleasure.

During the afternoon I went through all my slides for one of my most popular talks entitled 'How to grow 2,000 plants in a 20 x 30 foot garden'. I am funny about giving talks. Even if it is a talk that I am very familiar with, I always go through the slides to ensure they are the right way up, and facing the right way for projecting and that I know what I'm going to say about each one.

I then drove over to the Colchester Flower Club, where I received a very warm welcome and a cup of tea. This was even before I started my talk. I enjoyed presenting the talk, and I tried to make it relevant to the flower arrangers as well as the gardeners in the audience. They laughed at the bits they were supposed to and appeared to enjoy my commentary very much. Lots of people came and chatted to me after the talk, and I was given a lovely supper before returning home.

Being looked after properly when giving a talk is not rocket science, but it's surprising how often speakers like me do not receive a proper introduction, let alone a vote of thanks afterwards and are sent on our way without so much as a cup of tea. If you have just travelled for up to three hours to get to a hall, and then have to face a three-hour trip back, it's nice at least to be shown where the toilets are, and to be offered a little refreshment.

By contrast, I have been to halls where there were no facilities except the loo, but thoughtful ladies have come armed with a flask and some biscuits. Believe you me—it really does make a difference. Sometimes people just do not think about this courtesy, unless there is a person on the committee designated to looking after speakers.

*

5–6 September

Rupert and the crew wanted to follow me over the next two days, and film what I was up to.

I had returned to the garden in Waltham Cross that I had cleared previously, and spent the whole day sorting through plants that Mavis wanted to be planted out at the front.

I had prepared the beds by adding large amounts of well-rotted manure to try and increase the moisture retention. The soil is powdery dry. I also put on some fish, blood and bone fertilizer, as I felt that a slow-release organic fertilizer would be best in this garden. Fast-release fertilizers would not be retained in such powdery, dust-dry soil.

I put all the silver foliage plants, such as *Convolvulus cneorum, Stachys byzantina* and *Cerastium tomentosum,* together with pale blue flowering ones, which included *Campanula pulla, C. carpatica, C. cochlearifolia* and agapanthus, in a border which is in full sun all day. On the opposite side, where it is partly shaded for some of the day, I went for the whites and pale pinks provided by the osteospermums, blues of stokesia and several different iris species and then a touch of silver from *Artemisia schmidtiana*. By the end of the day I had fully replanted both borders and had watered everything in.

The following day I was round with Reg, picking plums to take to a friend who has a preserves stall at the Hertford farmers' market. She will make them into delicious jam.

Reg is so funny, when filming, and he still forgets not to make comments to the film crew. Every time he does so, Rupert tells him that to the viewer the crew are just not there, but Reg just does not remember. It starts me laughing and then have a job trying to recall what I was doing or saying. I must admit, Rupert has the patience of a saint with us all, as we certainly do not always do what he would like, or what he expects from us. I suppose that is the problem when filming real life rather than action that is scripted.

Once the crew had finished for the day, Reg and Pat invited me round for a snack. We took our seats on the patio, recalling the day's activity, and enjoyed the sunny evening over a bottle of wine. This was just the ideal way for me to wind down after two days of filming.

✳

7 September
I spent the day at the Byrkley Garden Centre near Burton-on-Trent. In the afternoon I carried out an autumn and winter hanging basket demonstration, and in the evening I gave a presentation on 'My

Life' as part of the Brighter Borough Presentation Evening held at the garden centre for the East Staffordshire Borough Council.

This was an evening honouring all those who had won awards in the gardening competitions in the borough. It was planned around a nice meal with wine, as well as my chat, and was most enjoyable. What is so obvious at such events is the vast talent and enthusiasm shown by gardeners, schools, pubs, community centres, sheltered homes and so on in creating a nicer and more colourful environment. I take my hat off to all the gardeners, around the country, who try so hard to make our island a more beautiful place in which to live. I sometimes think that gardeners only have private 'ownership' of their back gardens, whereas their efforts in their front gardens are shared with the local community and benefit many people other than themselves.

8 September

I was over at Buckhurst Hill again, in the garden of the block of flats. The task today was to weed the paths and edges of the buildings before putting down weed-killer to keep them clear and safe through the autumn and winter.

Once I got home again, I opened my e-mails to find one from BBC Worldwide. It turned out to be a rough idea for this book's cover. I was so thrilled by it. It used one of Howard Rice's very warm photographs showing my enjoyment of the garden and my life. He had been keen to capture the real Christine and had spent all day with me in different colours and positions in the garden.

When I had received a phone call to organize the photo-shoot, the commissioning editor spoke to me about sending a make-up person to do me up, and said that I should have my hair done. I spent a few seconds composing my reply. I said that I did not mind someone coming, but if, when I looked in the mirror, I didn't like what I saw, then off it would come. In the end she agreed with me that, if I felt I needed any when the photographer turned up, I would do it myself.

What did puzzle me about this request was that we are now on the second series of *Christine's Garden*, and in every single photograph I have had taken since the first series started, and throughout the filming, I have not worn any make-up at all. I know the editor has a job to do, but I don't think I look that bad without it, and I think the book cover is great even without the make-up and hairdo.

I very seldom wear make-up, so I decided I would wait and see if Howard made a comment. He was very particular that he wanted to show the real me, so he spent a lot of time with me and said he did not think it was needed. After all, *Christine's Garden* is about my life and me. If you meet me in the street, or even at a posh do, you are unlikely to see me wearing make-up. I believe in being true to myself.

*

9 September
I spent the morning taking some more of Reg's plums over to my friend Maya, who sells preserves at farmers' markets. She was at Hertford today and Rupert came along to film the event, with me tasting free samples and seeing how Maya was

getting on.

I first met Maya through the Action for Growth in the Rural Economy, an initiative of East Herts Council. I am a business development consultant for them, and was asked to go and see Maya to help her develop her Four Seasons Preserves business.

It was great and very satisfying to see that Maya had taken on so much of my advice, both in terms of display and labelling, and general business techniques. There's no doubt that I love cultivating people as well as plants. I get a great deal of satisfaction in seeing them both develop and bloom!

10 September

Penny came over to help me cut all the hedges at the back of the house. The garden slopes a lot and I do not feel safe up a ladder, on my own, when I have a mechanical trimmer in my hands. Penny comes over every year and helps me with this task. We collect all the clippings up and add them to my compost heap.

It was early evening before I set off for Lancaster in the car. This journey usually takes about four hours, but this time it took over six. There had been a fatal accident on the M6 and I sat for ages going nowhere. I eventually arrived at the hotel at midnight! I had hoped for an early night, because I was presenting a training day in the morning and these are always demanding and tiring. So much for planning.

11 September

I had been invited back to my old college, Myerscough, by a group of Lancashire farmers' market producers, to present a course on display and selling.

This is a very hands-on course, and I felt that the schoolchildren from Rose Bridge High School in Wigan might benefit from attending, as they will shortly be selling their own produce at a farmers' market in Bolton. I had a chat with the headmaster, who said he thought that both the children who had grown the produce, and some students who were studying graphic design, might benefit from attending.

I had never presented a course for both adults and children together, and I decided that the only way I could handle it was to get the adults to work with the children in small groups. I was pleased to see that this arrangement worked well and everyone enjoyed themselves. The children would come up with an idea, and then the adults would explain how it could work in practice. The adults and the children hadn't met before, but it was very satisfying to observe their enthusiasm and commitment to the course. At the end of the day the children left with a real buzz, and I was pleased that they had coped so well with what could have been a scary situation for them. They seemed to enjoy the tasting sessions the best, which was funny as I still like this bit in any course I run. Of course I have to try everything too, don't I, just to give them all encouragement!

*

12 September

I went up to Newnham College in Cambridge to be the instructor on a mower day. This is a day spent looking at the theory and practice of using both hand-operated and ride-on mowers.

I had six trainees, and we spent the morning learning about servicing and maintenance. Then, in the afternoon, I had them trying each of the machines I had available to use.

This is an interesting course, and one which always brings out the worst in some men, as you can see them thinking, 'What does she know?' I then have the satisfaction of seeing their body language and behaviour changing as I take them through such things as pre-start checks, servicing and the correct use of the machines. Normally, as the day goes on, it becomes apparent to all that I am there to help them overcome their bad habits, and get the best out of a machine.

Most of the less experienced trainees appreciate the opportunity to be shown how to use a machine, and then being allowed to use one in a safe environment where it does not matter if they make a mistake.

*

13 September

I was getting very behind in writing my weekly articles, so I spent the whole day producing six of them. Quite often I don't have a clue what I am going to write until I sit down to start, and then sometimes it comes straight away, but on other occasions I just don't seem to be able to actually make a start, and I end up doing everything else but write. By 8 p.m. I had managed to finish all six but I was shattered, so I had an early night and slept right through until 8 in the morning.

✱

14 September
This morning I spent time in the garden dead-heading, cutting back some unruly growth and mowing the lawn. I then set out for Penny's home where I dropped off Tara for the night before continuing on my way down to Fareham, in Hampshire. I had been invited by the organizers of the Fareham in Bloom Awards to give a presentation on 'My Life'.

People seemed interested in what I had done, they also laughed in all the right places and appeared to enjoy a well-organized event. As in Burton-on-Trent a week ago, lots of talented and committed gardeners were present, celebrating their achievements. It was a most enjoyable evening.

✱

15–17 September
Back home again, I spent time in my garden harvesting sweet corn, courgettes, carrots and pumpkins and lifting all my potatoes. Having done this, I then cleared the area and forked it over before sowing a green manure. This was a mixture of Italian ryegrass, mustard, red clover, winter tares and phacelia.

I sow green manure to protect the soil surface from heavy rain over the winter. It also helps keep all the plant nutrients in the top part of the soil where they are

242

needed. In the spring I will dig it in, to provide a source of organic matter.

College starts again next week, so I prepared some lecture notes and hand-outs. I have 65 students under my tutorial care and, because I am not only the lecturer but also the course manager for the four classes, this requires a lot of forward planning and organization. It certainly keeps me out of mischief during the winter months. I teach all day Monday, and then on Tuesday, Wednesday and Thursday evenings.

I gave time to thinking through the planting of 1,500 plants at Kirklees Light Railway, due to take place on Tuesday. I had to think about the best position for each batch of plants, and also what would be the best number of children for planting these. I was expecting about 80 children and about 20 adults.

*

18–19 September

On arrival at Kirklees I was informed that they hadn't obtained the tools and equipment needed for the planting, so I spent the afternoon with the manager shopping for trowels, buckets, rakes, watering-cans and trays to carry the plants up to the site.

Once I had obtained these, I spent the rest of the afternoon traying up the plants which had remained and been grown on at the site. This involved removing the weeds that had crept in, putting them into batches and then labelling them all.

By 6 p.m. Rupert and the gang had turned up

and we spent some time talking through, with the manager, what we hoped would happen the next day. We all went to see what had been achieved already by clearing the top of the line and what I was going to be dealing with.

The weather forecast was not good, and I spent much of the night thinking how I was going to motivate and organize 80 young children to plant 1,500 plants in the rain. I must say that it was causing me nightmares. I need not have worried, as I got up to a cold but fine day, with no rain to spoil our parade!

I had been apprehensive about this day for some time. Over the summer I had worried about how the young children were coping with looking after the plants that they had taken away. Would they remember to water the plants, would they repot them into a bigger pot if they needed it and, more importantly, would they bring them back alive and kicking?

Well, my fears were unfounded, as all but 73 plants made it though the summer. I think this was quite brilliant. To see youngsters walking towards the train, carrying plastic bags filled with their charges, filled me with delight and admiration. What little stars they all were.

To make things easier for myself, I had already put all the plants that remained on site into trays, so that the children could get them on to the train. But, when it came to lifting the trays, I realized I had filled them too full and had made them too heavy. Over the summer I had forgotten how small some of these children were.

What we did, therefore, was simply let the children carry what they could manage. Some took just two plants, others a full tray, and somehow all 1,500 plants ended up on the train, although I had absolutely no idea whereabouts.

On the way up to the end of the line I was thinking desperately about how I could organize getting the plants into their designated places. In the end I decided that the only way was to ask all the children to bring their plants to me in turn, and for me to place them where they needed to be.

I was extremely lucky that the sun shone, even though it was chilly, and that ten adults from Mires Beck Nursery, where I had obtained the young plants, said they would come over and help me plant. As it turned out, they were my saving grace. Once I had everything in place, they all mucked in with the children, showing them how to plant and helping them keep the spacing correct.

Everyone who put the plants in, children and adults alike, did a first-rate job. It was lovely to see children from different schools, and the adults from the nursery, all working together to achieve a common goal. When all the plants had gone in, the children watered them and, from the vantage-point of the train, I looked at the site and felt so proud. They had started a very important project that was going to change this bit of Yorkshire for ever, and I felt so pleased, despite being a Lancastrian!

*

20–22 September

I managed to write four more weekly articles and take photographs to support them. Often it is not the writing of short articles that is a problem, but getting suitable photographs to support what I have written. At least these days we have digital cameras. I find it amazing to be able to write about Reg, nip round to see him, take his photograph and then send the whole lot down the line. Such is technology.

I prepared a lot of teaching material this week, as I have a new group of RHS Level 2 students starting. There are 25 of them, including, to my surprise, more mature students than of late. I find that this type of student is frequently more dedicated than the younger student. They seemed a nice group, and at the end of the three-hour lecture several thanked me. This is always a good sign.

I also had a couple of long walks with Tara along our favourite bit of countyside by the river. I love this bit of countryside and seeing Tara run free. She recently seems to have had a second wind and has been walking better over the past three or four weeks. She does have problems lying down, but I think that this is due to rheumatism, and the vet does too. She still has a spark and enjoys life.

We love each other so much and she has been a great companion, always at my side giving me so much pleasure, love and company. She continues to be a great mate and I know how much it will hurt and how much I will miss her. I keep telling myself just to think of the lovely times we have had together, but somehow it does not really help.

✳

23 September
Over in Brentwood, at Tomlins Nursery, I was presenting, and taking part in, a gardeners' question time. I do enjoy these live sessions, where people bring samples to identify and problems to

solve.

We had pear rust again, the second time I have seen this rare disease this year; some apples that were so small they were really only good for making cider, so what could be done to make them bigger next season; several questions on how to deal with the pruning of clematis and a few on fruit growing, and problems such as powdery mildew and rust on various plants.

During the evening I drove up to Bolton. In the morning I'm going to a farmers' market to see how the children from Rose Bridge High School are getting on with their stall.

*

24 September

What stars these children are! When I saw them at their stall for the first time I filled up. I felt so very proud of them that tears came to my eyes.

It was great to think that they had constructed the growing beds themselves, had planted and raised the plants, had harvested them, boxed them and priced them up—and here they were, for the first time in their lives, selling produce they themselves had grown. They had told the teachers to clear off, as they wanted to do this final part on their own.

They had noted most of the things I had talked to them about on the farmers' market course that they had taken part in. They were wearing co-ordinated T-shirts, all printed with the same logo that was displayed on the stand, on paper carrier bags and on leaflets that the children were giving out to people who passed the stall.

They looked great, were speaking to people

nicely and with good manners, were not using calculators and, all in all, were having a great time. I felt so very pleased at their enthusiasm and so proud. I do not think I have ever felt so impressed by children's efforts before. These are children who, six months ago, had never been to a farmers' market or grown a plant.

I thought it was fantastic, really lovely to see. The children themselves, their parents, their school and everyone involved with them deserved to feel a great sense of achievement with what they had done. I was so happy for them, I did almost cry. I literally had to fight back the tears, or they would have been running down my face.

So much progress, so much achieved in such a short period of time. All by children from Wigan who probably would have never grown a thing while at school. But they had joined the new gardening group, set up by a caring and very aware headmaster and some of his staff, who had the vision to turn a playing field into a community growing space, not only for the children, but for their families as well.

Children who when I first met them were tongue-tied and shy, were now shouting out cries such as 'Buy one lettuce get one free—but not for teachers!' They even set up bargain bags towards the end of the sale to sell everything off, and they even walked around the market with these bags and sold them.

I saw enjoyment in the children's eyes, a great admiration from the headmaster and staff who attended, and I could not have been any happier. The thought that I had been a tiny part of this was unbelievable. I could not believe how happy I felt for them. They were stars that shone so brightly, on a very wet Lancastrian morning, that it was a joy to see.

I also couldn't help thinking of all those children who are not academically talented and are written off just because of this, or their background. I left school with no qualifications worth talking about, and did not like school much, so I know what it is like. My headmaster said I would never be short of cash, but would never make much of my life!

I sometimes feel that we adults do not try hard enough to find the things that will set a fire burning in the child. We are bound by restrictions on what we can and cannot do in our schools. I think we should look at the child and develop life skills, rather than just a set of paper qualifications.

I felt these schoolchildren had gained so many life skills through this project that they did not need a piece of paper. They are capable of getting on in this world and coping well. I smile every time I recall that first vision of them on their own stall. It was a sight to behold.

Since I was back in Lancashire, I decided it would be nice to return to Myerscough College and have a proper look round, as I didn't really have the time when I was there for the course the other week. It felt odd wandering round the glasshouse unit and grounds after 32 years. It was here that I learned so much that was to prepare me for my life.

I sat once again in the lab where I used to sit to be taught about botany and about pests and diseases, and looked back over the years. How could I have known what I was taking away from these walls and those teachers? I never dreamed while I was there that I would become a lecturer myself one day.

In the residential block where I had spent time living and studying, I re-lived the times I would climb out of the kitchen window with my six-week-old puppy so she could go for a pee. I had got her just when I was due to be finishing my course and would be moving on. I knew the parents of my puppy well and I really wanted to have her.

I decided that if she lived in the bottom drawer of my chest-of-drawers she would be safe and, if I left my radio playing while I was in lectures, no one would know about her. I know I had the cleaners on my side, but I cannot remember how that came about. I knew that if the matron found me with a puppy I would have been thrown out. I used to go back to her during breaks. It seems funny now to think that I had the nerve to do it, but at the time it seemed so right that I should have her.

*

25 September

Today I returned to Clitheroe Castle. This is where I started my first job after finishing school, with the Clitheroe Parks Department. I had not been back since leaving to go to Myerscough, as life has taught me that sometimes, when you return to a place, it has changed so much that the lovely memories that you had are destroyed.

My visit evoked mixed emotions. The glasshouses were now in ruins, as apparently the Parks Department is being moved to a new site. The castle keep and the surrounding buildings are going to be developed into an education centre. The mess room had been improved so much that most of what I remembered had gone. No cold tap and dirty sink, where I spent hours washing pots; no wood-burning stove that never made it right through the night, so it was always freezing cold when we arrived for work at 7.30 a.m.; and apparently no rats!

One of the bowling greens that I used to look after was just the same. The café, under which I use to store my mower, had been done up and now was serving a very reasonable lunch. Benches still surrounded the crown green where old men used to come and watch me struggle with a mower that was too big for a small girl. I had the strength then but not the height. I had to mow those greens until the lines were so straight and crisp it was untrue. It did, however, teach me how to use a mower, and I can still mow in straight lines after all these years.

Rather naughtily, I climbed on to the rock garden that I had planted with tulips some 32 years before, sat on the same rock where I had had my photograph taken, all those years ago, and looked down the High Street remembering the men that I had worked with. Mixed memories but, in the main, good ones.

From Clitheroe I drove up to Lancaster through the Trough of Bowland. I love this bit of Lancashire and always try to visit if I am up this way. I think it is one of the most beautiful places in the world.

*

26 September

Back home again, I was preparing for the evening meal. At the Bolton farmers' market I had bought a whole lot of Lancashire produce and was putting on a Lancastrian evening for Reg, Pat, Louise and

Colin. Elaine, who had looked after Tara for me while I was away, was bringing her home, so I asked her to join the gang.

We had black pudding, sausages, Lancashire hotpot, cheese and Chorley cakes along with sarsaparilla beer. I do not think Reg was too impressed with this beer, as he soon moved on to the real stuff. It was a nice evening, and I enjoyed reminiscing about my trip home.

✻

27–30 September

These were days for catching up with the e-mails and letters which had accumulated while I was away.

I went into the garden and spent time dead-heading, picking up fallen leaves and taking cuttings of fuchsias, geraniums, plectranthus and salvias so that they could over-winter in the cold frame. And I went round to Reg's for some plums and apples, which I cooked and stored in the freezer for the winter.

OCTOBER

1 October

A very wet and cold day, so I had a nice time reading magazine articles which I had previously flagged up, but had been too busy to read over the past couple of months. I try to keep up to date with what is going on in the horticultural industry, but I find it very difficult because of all the other demands on my time.

Between the heavy showers I took Tara across the fields for a walk, and collected some large flat mushrooms. I had these for my tea. I like them grilled whole, with fried leeks on top and a good strong cheese melted over them, accompanied by a nice glass of red wine. Despite the rain, I ended up feeling there was not too much wrong with the world!

*

2 October

I took the train into London to do a live radio broadcast on LBC with Anna Raeburn. We used to work together on another radio station in the past, so it was good to catch up and work with her once again.

She reminded me, and the listeners, of the first time we worked together. I had been due to broadcast at 1 p.m. and the regular presenter was having difficulty getting into the studio due to very heavy traffic. Eventually, at 12.55, the producer said to Anna that she would have to present the programme.

Anna was not totally happy about this, saying she knew very little about gardening. I replied, 'Don't worry, you do the people bits, and I will do the plants.' This seemed to make an impression on Anna and, even though we have not broadcast together for probably five years, she remembers my comments well.

I've often noticed how, in the world of radio, even though most people work together professionally enough, when the chemistry between two people really clicks, the programme can be pure magic.

Anna and I did not have to say anything to each other today before we went 'live', we just picked up from the previous occasion. I enjoyed the hour a lot and, judging by the laughter that came from Anna, I assume she and the listeners did as well.

I love doing live events, especially radio, talking to and helping individual people. I work on the basis that I am speaking to that person and that person alone. The fact that hundreds of other people are eavesdropping does not worry me.

We discussed ferns, badgers, re-seeding a lawn, red spider mites, shelter for a balcony, growing Japanese maples from seeds, how to start cultivating an allotment, orchids, rabbit problems, brambles, mildew on grapes and figs, tomatoes, fairy rings, sending seeds to Cyprus and runner beans. All in all it was a very nice mix.

*

3 October

I had a busy morning getting material ready for my college lectures during the rest of the week, and then drove over to Worcester. I had been invited to the 'Worcester in Bloom' and 'Worcester Allotment Forum' to present the prizes at their presentation evening.

I enjoyed this evening very much, and was surprised to hear my past college principal, Bill Simpson from Pershore College, introduce me in such glowing terms. He had obviously been following my career, as we had not seen each other for many years.

He acted as the master of ceremonies while I gave my talk on 'The making of *Christine's Garden*' and then I handed out the prizes and congratulated everyone. It was very impressive to see the photographs of the prize-winners, and it made one appreciate the hard work and effort that so many people had put into making their part of the country look so nice.

*

4 October

I returned home in the morning to be greeted by the film crew. Sarah, was going to have a go at directing me later in the day. She would be accompanied by David Evens acting as the cameraman as Rupert was up in Birmingham editing the first batch of the series. She shows promise and I think, with more experience, will make a great director. I appreciate her sense of humour and the fact that she is such a great cook! Not only is she talented in the world of TV production but also she makes food look and taste so nice.

I discovered early on that her role in the team is not only to help Rupert but also to ensure that we all eat at some stage in the day. Frequently, Sarah will produce a great lunch or supper. It must be nice to be so talented.

So Sarah and the team decided they would film me taking jam round to Reg. Maya had made this from the plums off his tree, which I gave her when I went to see her at the Hertford farmers' market. I gave the pot of jam to Reg, who opened it instantly, smelt it and then nearly tipped it all down himself—and followed this up with a comment about it not being very firm! I quickly suggested to Reg that he should pass the jam on to Pat, who said she would make some tea and toast.

What followed was very funny. Pat produced steaming cups of tea and some lovely toast spread with the jam, but when Reg was asked if he wanted to taste the jam, he said he did not want any, as it would spoil his tea! Needless to say, it did not take much to get him to sample the treat once he saw us tucking in.

In the evening I went over to college to lecture to my new students. They appear, at this stage, to be very keen and pleasant, with a nice mixture of ages.

*

5–6 October
I had a very difficult journey down to Sanders Garden World, near Bridgewater, in very heavy rain and appalling driving conditions. I eventually arrived with just enough time for a cup of tea and a sandwich before I presented a talk entitled 'A ramble through the potting shed'.

This is a chat about composts, fertilizers, feeding, liming, pH and so on. I know it sounds boring, but in practice it is probably the most fascinating talk I give, as it shows gardeners how to get the very best out of their soils to maximize productivity. I have yet to meet anyone who has not found the talk interesting and enjoyable.

After the talk, I was met by Andy and Rachel Doran who run the PR company which had organized my trip down to Sanders Garden World. They also accommodated me at their home overnight, and they took me out for an evening meal at a very nice pub close to where they live. This was so much nicer than staying on my own in yet another hotel. Instead I could just relax in their company and get to know them better, and I enjoyed the evening with them and their family very much.

The next day Andy drove me down to another garden centre, Trelawney & Ashford, near Barnstaple, where I repeated the talk. What was so nice about this venue was that so many people who had attended my chat in May turned up again, so it meant that the audience size had increased by about 100 per cent. The atmosphere was friendly and everyone asked lots of questions and enjoyed what I said. A cream tea rounded this off nicely! Andy then drove me back to Sanders Garden World to pick up my own car for the journey home. I was very tired by the time I got there.

*

7–8 October
The weekend was spent in my own garden. I removed the mildewed courgettes, harvested the last of the tomatoes and runner beans and finally took up the last of the potatoes, which I had left in the ground, as it was so dry.

Once I had cleared all the old crops, composted non-diseased material and taken down the runner bean supports, I forked over the ground and sowed some green manure. I always tend to sow green manure right into the autumn if it is warm enough for it to germinate.

It is a good source of organic matter, and helps prevent the heavy winter rains from destroying the soil surface over winter.

On the Saturday evening I drove over to see Geoff and Julia, two of my past students, who are developing a large garden. I had arranged to stay the night so that I could enjoy the evening meal with them and allow myself a drink. It was lovely just being able to sit and chat and not have to think of driving the 50 miles home.

Having been so busy this year, I appreciate my social time even more, and these rare opportunities just to sit quietly and chat in the company of friends have become very special occasions.

*

9 October

The crew turned up to film me working in my garden. Rupert was not with them, so we had David Evans as our cameraman again. Sarah was directing again so that she could gain more experience.

I just dead-headed flowers that needed my attention, mowed the grass and cut back a viburnum to shape, with Sarah directing questions at me as I worked. At one stage I asked her how many times she was going to ask me the same question! Eventually, I think about the seventh occasion of asking, she got an answer out of me which she liked.

This is the technique that we have developed. As I have said, occasionally, as today, it begins to get to me. However, if Rupert or Sarah persists and keeps asking the same questions time and time again, it usually results in my coming out with some 'treasure' in the end. It is just a very demanding method to extract something they do not even know they want! Sometimes I am lucky and give it to them first time round.

✱

10 October

I returned to Highgrove Garden Centre, in Kent, to carry out an autumn container and hanging basket demonstration. I gave two demonstrations during the day, which were attended by about 200 people. After I had finished, the bulbs sold really well, and it was very satisfying to see people going into the plant area to buy the plants that I had used in the demonstrations, and to ask me questions about what would be suitable in their own gardens.

Returning home in the late afternoon, I had something to eat and then left for college to lecture to my second-year students.

✱

11 October

Today I felt a great sense of achievement as I collated all the photographs for inclusion in this book and sent off the majority of the manuscript (nine month's worth) to the publisher! I cannot stand being late with anything, and on this occasion I had managed to submit ahead of my copy deadline. I wanted to do this, as I was going away for a few days later in the month, and did not want to have to worry or think about the book, or anything else to do with work, for that matter. I am very tired at the moment, and I just want a rest and to be quiet and not to have to do a lot. I only hope that what I have written will be OK.

It may sound strange, but I have found it hard work writing about my daily life. I suppose it is just because I have already done it, and lived it, so it hasn't been easy to be disciplined and keep details of what I have been up to, in detail, on a daily basis.

I write a diary every night, and have done so for more years than I can remember, but recording daily activity for this book has been another thing. I am pleased that the majority of the work is done. I have been working flat out for most of the year and I really need a break. I am due to submit my account of the remaining three months' activities in January.

*

12 October
I spent the day out in the front garden pruning back the long growths that the magnolia has produced since we have had some rain. I took all the long growths back to two buds, which I hope will be sufficient to ensure that I get some flowers in the spring. I have never pruned it this late before, so it is a case of 'time will tell'.

I removed the spent marigolds, which have finished flowering, and other annual bedding plants

260

which looked tired, and replanted with some wallflowers. All that could be composted was taken up and put into the bins, and any rubbish was put in the council recycling bin.

I spent a bit of time hand weeding the pavement to remove weed seedlings and pruned back the flat-growing juniper to give me a bit more room when I am sweeping up.

*

13 October

Our final day of filming for this series, and I must admit I am relieved. I am very tired, and the last few occasions when the crew have been down here have been more and more exhausting.

Don't get me wrong, I enjoy filming, but once I get very tired I find everything so much harder. I am very aware that I need a break, and not just a weekend. A bit longer than that. I need time for me.

Rupert was back with the team to capture my last comments of the season about my feelings in my garden. When they arrived they gave me some flowers and a present. My birthday is coming up, and they knew they would not be seeing me then.

I just love flowers, but most people never think of sending them to me as they are sure I have enough around me. I happened to mention this once to Rupert during a chat while putting the first series together, and he obviously remembered it. Now, on special occasions, when the doorbell goes and a florist is standing at the door with flowers, I know they can only be from Rupert or a close friend of mine. They always make me smile and leave me thinking how enjoyable it must be to be a

261

florist, who takes lovely flowers to people on a daily basis.

14 October

Today was a restful day just carrying out odd jobs out in the garden. I removed all the plant saucers from underneath the pots and replaced them with pot feet or stones to keep the pot off the ground over the winter.

This allows any water to drain freely through the pot, and in freezing weather water is able to escape instead of staying in the pot and causing the roots to rot on frozen ground.

I also took Tara for several short walks around my home. The autumnal colours are not really apparent yet. We need some cold and frosty weather to induce a change, but it was nice to be in the countryside with Tara and feel that sense of space and freedom.

A bit of time was spent round with Pat and Reg, drinking tea and discussing what Reg should be doing in his garden. He has already removed a lot of his tired bedding plants and trimmed his shrubs to shape, so he really just needs to tidy up.

15 October

I spent the entire day writing articles for publication over the next few weeks. I have managed to produce six, which means that I can send both my editors enough articles so that I can go away without having to worry about meeting deadlines.

Some days like this I can come up with article after article. On other days I struggle to keep focused on what I am supposed to be doing and get distracted easily. Then, I find it easy to make the excuse that Tara needs yet another walk, so off I go for an hour when really I should be working.

*

16 October

A lovely warm day in which I mowed my grass and trimmed to shape a viburnum and a vestia, and cut out the dead wood that had been left earlier in the summer.

The doorbell went and it was Louise, wanting to know if I was doing anything at lunch-time. When I asked why, she explained that as I would be away on my birthday, she and Reg, Pat and Colin wished to take me out for lunch. I said that would be lovely.

We all went to a pub just up the road and had a lovely meal, and then came back and sat on Reg's patio. It was warm, so we all decided we should make the best of the sunshine, as we would not have many more opportunities of enjoying each other's company in the open air once the weather changed.

*

17 October

I went over to Buckhurst Hill to carry out some maintenance in the grounds of the flats. This consisted of mainly weeding and removing some very old aster plants. These had grown so woody that they had started to look a mess, and several residents had asked if I would remove them.

In the evening I went over to college to lecture to my students on vegetable production.

*

18 October

Today I started to bring in some of the plants in the garden that are not reliably hardy, and would be damaged if we had a frost. These included fuchsias, and some of the geraniums, abutilons and petunias that I over-winter.

This involved cleaning the pots, checking to see if the plants have any pests or diseases on them, removing these if necessary, pruning back any excessive growth and just tidying them up. Most of the plants come inside and they sit on my large dining-room table which, at this time of the year, is pushed up against the French windows to try and ensure that the plants get enough light through the dark winter days.

To prevent any water damaging the table, I cover it with a large sheet of heavy-duty polythene before I put the plants on it. I admit it does not look that nice, but I do not have a greenhouse in which to over-winter things, and already all the windowsills in the house are covered in small pots. These contain cuttings which I over-winter and then take more cuttings from once they start into growth in the spring.

*

19–26 October

Away at last! I have been so looking forward to being away from the phone and work. I just want to

264

enjoy being with Tara and my friend, Penny, and her puppy, Indie.

We had rented a cottage near Grange-over-Sands, which belongs to my old college lecturer, Ben Andrews. I used to stay in this cottage when I was a student at the Lancashire College of Agriculture (now called Myerscough), but I had not been back to it in 30 years. It had changed a bit, with the addition of more rooms and a garage, but fundamentally it was just the same.

Before calling in on Ben and Susan to collect the keys, we got off the M6 at Preston and made our way to Garstang through the Trough of Bowland. Penny had never seen this very special area before, so it was lovely to share it with her. It also gave us the opportunity to give the dogs a good walk before we got to Ben's house.

Ben and Susan had invited us to stay for tea when we picked up the key, and it was lovely to see their garden again and get up to date with each other's news. We chatted about the 'open garden' they had enjoyed visiting in the summer, and their family, while I brought them up to speed with details of all the filming that had taken place this year. They had both featured in the first series, so they were keen to know what we had been up to while filming the second one.

The next few days were spent walking the dogs along numerous beautiful footpaths surrounding the cottage, and visiting a few gardens which were beginning to show the first signs of autumnal colour.

At Holker Hall the tree I admired most, in its autumn livery, was an *Oxydendrum arboreum*, with the common name sourwood. It's a tree from eastern North America which needs acid conditions. It was turning the most beautiful shades of red and, especially when illuminated by the sun's rays, it looked great.

The best garden, however, was that of the home of the Lakeland Horticultural Society at Holehird. It was looking fantastic, just aglow with autumn colours. The cornus and *Euonymus alatus* lit up their planting positions so well, whilst the sorbus and cotoneasters were dripping in berries. The views down to Lake Windermere were out of this world, as was the surrounding countryside.

A trip up to Wast Water allowed us to visit the sea, and exercise the dogs on the way there, before driving inland to the lake. The real beauty of this lake is the scree tumbling right down into the water. On a still day the reflections are breathtaking. The hawthorns in the hedges were turning that lovely burnt red, as they do before the leaves fall, and the berries almost looked like glow-worms in the mists of the early mornings. The little local church is the home to several graves of climbers who, over the years, have lost their lives on these magnificent hills and mountains. It serves as a reminder that Mother Nature should be treated with considerable respect.

We spent an interesting day at the Leighton Moss and Morecambe Bay nature reserves run by the RSPB. I had just got out of the car when a chap said to me, 'Hello, Christine. You don't know me, but I am your brother's next-door neighbour.' What the statistical chances are of this happening, I have no idea, but it did surprise me. He said he recognized me from the telly!

Penny and I had a great day and saw a red deer

grazing on the edge of reed beds near one of the hides. This was a lovely sight, especially as neither of us had seen one before. We were also treated to wigeons, shovelers, greenshanks, redshanks, lapwings and grey herons; coal, marsh, long-tailed and blue tits; teal, mallard, red-breasted merganser, pochard and pied wagtails.

I know that bird fanciers will not be particularly impressed with this list, but it does represent a substantial increase in my ability to identify birds. It is only in the past few years that I have started to learn their different features. They are so much harder to recognize than plants, as they often do not stay around long enough to allow you to take in all the detail that you need to be able to identify them.

On the trip back down south we called in to see my family. I do not get up to see them as often as I should, so I took the opportunity of calling. We chatted about what we had done during our stay at the cottage, discussed the second series of *Christine's Garden* and generally caught up on family news. We then had a very long journey home due to accidents, hold-ups and the sheer volume of traffic. I eventually got back to my place at about 9 p.m., not in the best frame of mind.

*

27 October

I spent the whole day with the news editor and a photographer from *Amateur Gardening* magazine. We decided we would go off into the Essex countryside and visit a few gardens to get some autumn colour shots. Unfortunately, because it was late in the season, it was bitterly disappointing. We did get a few shots, which will do to complement what I write about over the next few weeks, but there was not a lot of autumnal colour.

*

28 October

I cleaned my patio thoroughly today, which involved moving all my pots and containers and sweeping behind them. Over the summer, leaves and other rubbish build up behind them, providing the ideal over-wintering site for problems such as vine weevil.

I tidied all the pots by weeding them and cutting out any weak, damaged or diseased material, and ensured that all the drainage holes at the bottom of the pots were clear.

I decided which of the remaining plants in the garden were going to come into the house for the winter, and started to bring these in. The list included plectranthus, begonias, geraniums, my devil's tongue and aeonium. I have put the larger pots in my cold frame and mini plastic greenhouse, which are against the house wall. Given a normal winter, most things will come through with this amount of protection.

If it gets very cold I will also line the insides with bubble polythene and drape fleece over the plants.

To get up all the fallen leaves, I used the mower with the collection box on. I find this a very easy method of picking up the leaves. It also shreds them and mixes them with the grass clippings, which is an ideal combination for the compost heap.

∗

29 October

I spent much of the day writing, and ended up producing an article on early- and winter-flowering clematis. I am sometimes surprised at the amount I manage to write, as I often think I will not have enough to say but, a few hours later, I have managed to produce enough to fill a few columns.

In the evening I went round to see Reg and Pat and we enjoyed cheese and biscuits and a bottle of wine. I chatted about what Penny and I had done while we were away and got up to date with Reg and Pat's news. I do love spending time with them both. I am never fully sure why Reg and I laugh so much, but we seem to bring out the best, or funniest, side of each other. Pat just looks on and laughs with us.

∗

30 October

I went to college to start off a new group of daytime RHS Level 2 students. They are a very pleasant bunch, with a nice mix of ages, but with more women then men.

I carried out all the normal enrolment stuff, and then took them for a walk around the college campus to show them all the facilities we have, before getting started on botany.

This gave them their first glimpse of what the rest of the course would be like, and by the end of the day they all looked a bit shell-shocked. I did point out that it is an examination class and would be delivered as such, but I think several went away wondering what had they let themselves in for. Time will tell if they turn up next Monday!

In the evening Rupert phoned to let me know that the BBC was thinking of showing the first series of *Christine's Garden* again before Christmas. This pleased me, as it means that they actually think it is OK. I felt rather flattered as I called it a day.

*

31 October

I spent the morning on administration tasks in my office, and then the afternoon visiting a lady in Wood Green who wanted some advice on her garden.

She needs a lot of both hard landscaping and soft landscaping work carried out and did not know which to tackle first. I explained that the former, which includes the laying down and re-positioning of paths, creating standing ground for a shed and having an apron laid around the base of the house, will cause considerable upheaval. Therefore it will be better to get all that side of things organized and completed before thinking about which plants to put in where.

The garden is very large, and I explained that for her to have the garden changed in the manner she wants, with raised beds and terracing, she will need to get a professional person in to ensure that any retaining walls are well constructed and of the correct type.

In the early evening the project editor for this book phoned me to give me some feedback on the portion of the manuscript I had submitted so far.

Her comments were most encouraging and came as such a relief. I had spent a lot of time typing it in my two-fingered manner, and was getting concerned that what I had done so far might not be what was wanted. So to hear her words gave me considerable relief. It still took a bit of time before I started feeling really pleased.

NOVEMBER

1–2 November

The morning was spent on office work, sorting out my end-of-month finances and sending out invoices. I like doing this, because it makes my efforts of the past month as a self-employed person seem worthwhile. I remember my brother saying to me once that it must be odd not to receive a wage slip every month. I told him I did receive one, but it was in the form of cheques.

I gave a lecture to a local University of the Third Age gardening group on 'The making of *Christine's Garden'*. This is an interesting talk for me to give as each time I seem to remember something different. I hardly ever lecture from notes, so I suppose that different things will come to mind on different occasions.

On both evenings I was over at college lecturing to my students on outdoor vegetable production and the classification system used to name plants. Students find this great fun as I use my own family and their features to illustrate a point.

I often say that you cannot fail to spot a member of the Walkden family in a crowd of people as we all are small, have big bums, are on the well-built side (some people would say fat, but I am being kind to myself and my family members) and have a nose that you could plant potatoes with! At least it gets a laugh and does illustrate a point.

✳

3–5 November

I drove over to see my old friends Carol and Steven in Witney. The last time I saw them, in August, they invited me to their annual bonfire party and barbecue, a shared event for all the residents of The Close where they live.

When I arrived late Friday afternoon, Steven told me that I was joining them both round at friends in The Close that evening, to have a champagne tasting. I thought this sounded great fun.

I have, over the years, got to know most of the people living in the close, and everyone makes me very welcome when I'm there with Carol and Steven. The story behind the champagne was that Gill and Peter's son is getting married next year, and they wanted a consensus of opinion on which champagne to buy.

Several friends were invited, and after we had sampled three wines we were asked to make our decision. This was a light-hearted affair, but it was an interesting experience to be able to sample three together and note the difference. Fortunately, most of us picked the same one as being the nicest.

During the tasting, Reg's number one fan turned up, having returned from Sheffield University for the weekend. Aisha had taken a real shine to Reg during the first series, so I'd asked Reg if he would sign a photograph of himself for her. Reg, being the great chap he is, signed it 'To Aisha with love from Reg'. The thought of Reg being a pin-up at the age of 83 kills me!

Carol, Steven and myself left early, as Carol had cooking a lovely meal of roast beef with all the trimmings and had invited her immediate neighbour John round to join us. Carol is a great cook and always goes to a lot of effort to make really nice meals for me when I visit.

We had a very enjoyable meal, chatting about what we all had been doing since last we saw each other and also about the theatre, films and actors. The neighbour, John, fascinatingly recalled the first time he saw Shirley Temple!

Much of the weekend was spent getting everything ready for the party. A metal coal bunker was brought out, so that all the fireworks could be stored safely. Buckets were filled with sand and soil for letting off the rockets correctly, hose-pipes were laid out and first aid kits located. Barbecues were cleaned and put into position, and tables and chairs appeared in the roadway.

The residents of The Close are old hands at street party events, and these do's are always well attended and create a great sense of community spirit. Everyone contributed food, wine, beer and fireworks, and it was a really nice evening. We watched fireworks for about an hour, then we all started to get cold so we retreated into Anne and David's for drinks.

Before I returned home, Carol and Steven took me out for Sunday lunch and we were joined by Carol's mum, Grace, who has to be Reg's number two fan! For me, one of the nicest things that have come out of *Christine's Garden* is seeing how much fun and pleasure being on the TV has given Reg, and for that matter Pat.

Everywhere I go people ask about Reg. I hear things like 'How are Reg, Louise and Tara?' and 'I think the programme is lovely.' Reg and Pat get stopped and spoken to regularly, and will even give an autograph if asked. I think it's fantastic that the public have taken to Reg as much as I have. After all he is one of the nicest chaps I know, and he's just great on TV.

*

6 November
The day was spent at college lecturing on the parts of the plant. We looked at the stem, leaf and roots, and then moved on to investigate flower structure by pulling apart some flowers to show the students all the component parts.

Next, I set my students an exercise in which I asked them to look at ten plants and identify the type of margin, tip, base and outline shape shown by the leaves. This made the students look very closely at the leaves to spot the sometimes very small differences.

Later in the day we started to look at seed structure and germination, and the conditions required for seed germination.

It is only the second time these students have been with me, and they are having to get accustomed to studying hard for seven hours at a time. I do vary things a lot, but I take my hat off to these particular students, who are managing to concentrate for a long periods. They appear to enjoy my style of lecturing but, I must admit, I am quite a hard taskmaster.

*

7–8 November
I spent a lot of time sorting out the handouts needed for my college students for the rest of the

term. I have to give my requests for photocopying to the administrative staff at least a week in advance. Because I lecture to four different groups of students, it takes a quite a bit of organizing to ensure that all goes smoothly.

I also got everything together for the coming weekend. I am leading a garden tour in the Cotswolds, in which we will be looking at late autumnal colour, and, as a precaution, I phoned each of the gardens to check that they know we are visiting and contacted the coach company to see that all was well with them.

I attended a good lecture at college which was given by Chris Beardshaw about planting and environmental issues. He was both informative and entertaining and raised some interesting points. I do not often get time to attend other speakers' lectures, so it made a very pleasant change to have an opportunity to listen instead of presenting for once.

I went into college during the evenings to lecture to my students on seed germination, flower structure, pollination and fertilization. I am beginning to get the impression that my new starters are settling into their new routine very well and are enjoying coming to the classes as we seem to spend a lot of time laughing.

*

9 November
I drove into Surrey to talk once again about the making of *Christine's Garden*. This was to raise funds for the Lifetrain Trust which supports young, disabled people and helps them to make positive changes in their lives.

276

I enjoyed the day, and chatting to the various members of the committee and the audience. It struck me that there was a lot of hard and dedicated work being done by this organization.

The evening was spent over at college with my RHS Advanced Certificate students, looking at tree and shrub production.

10 November
I took Tara over to my friend Penny for the weekend. I then drove on to Bourton-on-the-Water, in the Cotswolds, to lead the autumnal colour weekend. I arrived in time to chat to the manager of the house that the tour company own about the weekend, and meet the other tour leader, who was doing a William Morris weekend. We spent the afternoon talking to people as they arrived, and then, after dinner, we split into our separate groups. I introduced the weekend and the gardens which we are going to visit and spent time answering the inevitable questions about *Christine's Garden*.

11–12 November
We went off in our coach to Batsford to visit the arboretum (which means a collection of deciduous trees), and saw some lovely acers and fantastic sorbus in fruit. Standing next to a lovely coloured prunus I said to my group, 'I have a tip for you', and the lady next to me, who was a real character with a terrific sense of humour, immediately replied, 'So it's called tipfea.' Just goes to show the

problems some people can have with a Lancastrian accent! Still, it gave everyone a laugh and it did provide me with an amusing plant name to look for over the weekend. I suppose this could be how wrong plant names are sometimes invented.

In the afternoon we made our way towards Oxford and the gardens at Waterperry. This was a big disappointment, as they had experienced rain and frost recently, and I have to say that everything was looking miserable, with no colour really to talk about.

After we had spent just an hour there I decided I needed to take the group somewhere else. By this stage it was getting cold and grey. so I thought the best place would be a local garden centre which is known for its excellent Christmas displays, coffee shop, large car park, clean toilets—and which would accept a group with prior booking. Such contingencies have to be thought about when leading garden tours. When things need changing it is not always possible to drop into the first place you think of, because the groups tend to be large in number and we often have to phone ahead to get permission for the coach.

At the house in the evening I conducted a gardeners' question time, which the whole group attended. This was great fun, with questions such as 'How do plants get their names?', 'How does someone like me remember them all?', 'What are the best plants for a shady, north-facing border?', 'What should be done about black spot on roses?', 'What can you do about fairy rings on lawns?', 'What winter protection should you give to plants growing in California?'—which is where one of the guests came from. Things over there are very different from here, and I was glad that I had some experience of that part of the world, so I was able to help her.

The following day broke sunny but chilly, and we set off to the Nation's Arboretum at Westonbirt. This has been a favourite place of mine ever since Ben Andrews, first took me there as a student over 30 years ago. We went to see the famous acers which were ablaze with colour.

I always describe these trees within the glades as looking as if someone has poured petrol underneath them and set them on fire. They radiate their glowing rich reds, purples, ambers, coppers and golds with such intensity that it looks as if the area's in flames.

We spent the whole day there, which is not a problem as they have 17 miles of pathways, and the site is divided into the old section and a newer section in which the acers were looking out of this world. The autumnal sun shone, and the entire group had a fantastic day. We got back to the house in time for a lovely cream tea, including not only traditional scones, jam and cream but also other delicious items, some of which I enjoyed before my return home.

∗

13 November
I was at college all day lecturing on the botanical parts of flowers, the movement of water in plants and the use of plant growth regulators in horticulture. Students generally seem to find lectures on the use of chemicals interesting, and I always try to explain the advantages and well as disadvantages associated with their use. I like to

think they are made aware of a lot of the issues surrounding this topic.

*

14 November

I spent the day over at a place called Little Cambridge, near Dunmow in Esssex, stripping out an overgrown bed of flowers and shrubs. This involved cutting down shrubs which had grown to 3m (10 feet) high, with a similar spread, digging out the roots and then removing all the material to the far end of the garden. The border is on a heavy clay, so it was hard work, not assisted in any way by rain which, in the end, came down so heavily that I would have done more harm than good if I had continued. It would have to be finished another day.

*

15 November

I had a lovely drive over into Bedfordshire to see my friend Gill, whom I had not visited for a while. The trip over there was great.

Several frosts had worked their magic on the trees, which were erupting into some of the best autumn colour we have seen around here in a while. The beech trees just glowed like amber beacons along the roadside, and these contrasted so well with the red berries of the hawthorn and mountain ash. It was lovely.

After lunch Gill and I went for a lovely walk along

the river that flows along the back of her home. I wished Tara had been there, as she would have loved seeing Gill and all the ducks. I hadn't taken her with me, as Gill's partner is not very keen on dogs, but he was out on this occasion so it would not have mattered.

In the evening I went over to college to lecture on botany to my students.

*

16 November

I was due to return to the garden where I had been working the day before yesterday, but it was again raining so hard that there was no point. I took the opportunity to get up to date with magazine and other articles and in the afternoon I decided to give my houseplants a tidy. I removed old, damaged foliage, pruned out over-vigorous growth and cleaned the pots, adding fresh soil in some of the pots where the compost had shrunk. I have over 200 plants inside the house at this time of the year, so it is always a time-consuming job, and this was an opportunity too good to miss.

*

17 November

The morning was spent preparing a lecture entitled 'Plants for difficult places' for a University of the Third Age group in Theydon Bois. Bettie, a friend of mine, lives near the hall where I was going to be speaking, and she invited me round for lunch before the talk. I had not seen her for some time, so it was nice to hear about all her activities. Like a lot of my friends, she was a student of mine some 25 years ago. Thinking about that does start to make me feel old, as I really do not feel as if I have been at it that long.

After a lovely lunch I delivered the talk, which was well received and created a lot of laughter. I enjoy making people laugh. It must be great being a comedian and having that spontaneous ability to make an audience erupt into laughter. I always feel happy if my audience laughs when I'm giving a talk and at least I know they are not asleep!

I managed to watch the first programme of the repeat showing of *Christine's Garden*. This time round I was nowhere near as critical, and actually enjoyed the programme for what it is. The first time I was unsure what to think about it all. It is very strange seeing yourself as others do. I do think Reg is such a star. He adds so much to the programme, and it makes me even more pleased to think that he is actually my neighbour. I am a very lucky person.

∗

18 November
A beautiful autumn morning, and I just had to get out and walk Tara.

> *There are times when I must experience that feeling of a crisp, cold autumnal wind on my face, the exhilaration of a vast landscape releasing energy and the sheer wonderment of nature.*

After returning home, I opened my e-mails to find that there were 246 of them, all commenting on *Christine's Garden*. I did not expect anyone to watch it, as it was competing with *Children in Need*

282

and *Coronation Street*. However, judging from my e-mails, I was wrong.

The e-mails made me smile this time round. Their comments were warm, sincere and very complimentary, just as last time, but this time haven't reduced me to tears. I suppose I was just too close to it before, and worried about the content of the programmes, so my tears were partly ones of relief. Today I can fully appreciate the kind words in the manner in which they are meant. How time changes things!

*

19 November

The students at college have invited me to take part in a series of evening lectures about plants. They have asked me if I will talk about my travels, and I have decided to put together a completely new talk highlighting places like North America, which a lot of people think is not that good for plants. I plan to show them just how rich a flora can be found in the coastal mountains of both the east and the west.

I spent most of the day working on this. I have selected slides from numerous trips, and put them together carefully so that they will flow well on the night. It always surprises me just how long it can take to put a new lecture together; it's often several hours before I am comfortable with what I am going to be showing. It is lovely being asked to talk specifically about plants. I can really indulge in what I most enjoy.

*

20 November

In college all day today, and my new first-year students were keen to talk to me about *Christine's Garden*, having seen it on Friday evening. Some had seen it for the first time, while others had watched it again and said that they got more out of it a second time, when they were listening to what I was saying rather than just watching me. They made very nice comments, and I spent a lot of time answering their questions about the making of a television series before getting down to the subject in hand.

*

21 November

I collected up the leaves which had fallen into the front garden, and I will dig them into the vegetable patch in the spring.

I often not only collect the leaves which fall in my garden, but will go down the street and collect the ones lying in the gutters. I have this thing about organic matter and, because I cannot get enough of it, I am a bit of a scavenger at this time of the year.

The rest of the day was spent writing new lecture material for college and preparing a training course which I will be deliver in the new year.

*

22–23 November

I returned to the garden in Little Cambridge to continue to remove overgrown trees and shrubs.

284

This was proving a difficult task, as the shrubs had been there a long time and some of the roots took a lot of getting out.

Once I had removed the roots, I left the site because rain was falling very heavily and I did not wish to destroy the soil structure by walking all over it when it was too wet.

Back home, I worked on the planting plan, and then went over to Langthorns Plantery in Essex to source what I needed. With its helpful and approachable staff, I find this an excellent place to obtain plants.

*

24 November

I spent most of today working on a new format for my articles in *Amateur Gardening*. They have asked me to write more about what I am doing on a daily basis, and to try and include practical tips for the reader. I do find it difficult to obtain photographs that will work well with the articles. The problem is basically that I can't take photographs of myself, but I am sure that in the long term I'll be able to find a solution to this—either by asking someone to take a photograph of me or by getting a tripod and putting on the timer.

*

25 November

I drove over to the BBC radio studio in Chelmsford to take part in *Down to Earth* with Ken Crowther. This is a two-hour live phone-in show where we take any questions that come our way. Today's subjects included pruning a wisteria, bay trees, grapes, evergreen shrubs, how to control moles, camellia producing seed, taking conifer cuttings, what to do with date palms over winter, how to grow plants in containers with no soil, growing orchids, ginger and magnolias, how to move a skimmia at this time of the year and what to do with cannas.

It was a lively programme, which was presented by Mike Kelly today as Ken has a sore throat and cold. I have worked with Mike in the past and we get on very well, so the change of presenter did not throw me.

I spent the rest of the day getting everything ready for college next week.

*

26 November
I went over to see Bella D'Arcy and her partner, John. It was a special birthday for John, and Bella had invited a few other friends over to help him celebrate. We all had a lovely meal together, chatted away about past times and just relaxed amongst good company.

*

27 November
I was in college with the Monday group. They started learning about soils, and I could see that they were fascinated by the subject. I love the way the students' attitude changes before my eyes. Over a matter of a few weeks, I see them becoming more interested, enquiring, thinking about what is being said to them and questioning their own experiences. I love it. Helping to develop people's minds is one of the thrills of teaching.

In the evening I went round to find out how

Louise had got on with a job interview. She had been apprehensive about it, having not had an interview for a number of years, but she seemed very positive about the experience. From what she said I think she gave it her best shot, and only time will tell. I then nipped in to see Pat. Cataracts had developed in both her eyes over the previous years and she had been to the hospital to see about having them removed. I wanted to find out how her day had gone.

It turned out that one eye can wait, but the other needs doing as soon as possible. But all is well and she is now on the waiting list.

28 November
Rain still prevented me from returning to the garden at Little Cambridge, so I worked all day in the office, clearing my paperwork, e-mails and letters.

In the evening I went over to college to complete outdoor cut flower production with my Advanced Certificate students.

29 November
The project editor for this book came to see me to chat over editorial queries and to show me the first layouts and photographs. Fortunately for me, there were not too many queries and, in two hours, we had made the alterations needed up until the end of June. The remaining part of the book will be sorted out at a later date. From what I have seen so far, I am pleased with the suggested format and layout.

After lunch I went for a walk with Tara and could not help admiring the oak trees still holding on to their burnt brown leaves. A lot of the other trees have now dropped their leaves, but the oaks still have their clothes on.

I really enjoy looking at the naked skeletons of trees in winter. I have always liked seeing silhouettes against winter skies. I remember the skyline from my allotment as a kid, and looking up to see what I used to call my guardian angels—vast trees looking down on me from the hill-tops. In some ways I think they are at their most vulnerable, but also their most elegant, at this time of the year.

I watched a blue tit playing in the hedgerow and, as it flew off, admired its front plumage which seemed to be the same blue colour as the sky. It was a warm and sunny day for this time of the year, and I was just enjoying walking in the countryside seeing what nature was up to.

The rest of the day was spent answering my e-mails and getting things ready for tonight's class. I was covering the vegetative parts of the plant, so students will be chopping up things like rhizomes, stolons, bulbs and corms and learning why each of these items is so called. I enjoy this practical session as it really makes the students think very hard about what they have learned to date.

*

30 November

Today I went into London to attend the Garden Writers Awards Lunch at the Savoy Hotel. I had been invited by Westland's, one of the companies that make compost, and was pleased to be attending. Like the Oscars, this is an event where people's talent and skills are recognized by fellow professionals in the media world.

First there is a champagne reception, then a three-course lunch and finally the awards ceremony itself. There are sixteen categories, celebrating the best in television, writing, broadcasting and photography.

The event was very enjoyable, and it is always interesting to see who wins. The BBC won the 'TV Broadcast of the Year' award for *The Gardener's Year* for the fourth time in five years. This is some record, and confirms the level of professionalism that I have experienced for myself over the past two years.

I got back home just in time for a snack before going over to college to lecture on trees.

DECEMBER

1–2 December

The soil in the borders and vegetable area is too wet for me to be doing anything out in the garden at the moment. In these conditions I am a great believer in leaving things alone. As I've said before, by walking on wet soil you destroy the structure of it, and it can take years to re-form. It is much better to wait for conditions to improve.

I have spent these two days writing articles and completing the November section of this book.

I broke the day up by taking Tara for a walk. I noticed that the oak trees are still holding on to their leaves. This is unusually late, and I wonder when they will eventually fall. Almost all the other trees are bare now, and I will spend the next few months enjoying the naked trunks of trees and their silhouettes against winter skies.

*

3 December

I received my first Christmas card with mixed feelings as this always sends me into a wild panic. I write hundreds of cards and never seem to start them soon enough. This time of the year always seems to creep up on me and, before I know it, Christmas Day is here.

I spent most of the day writing exam questions for my students and preparing a new lecture entitled 'Plants from around the world'.

Some months ago I had a phone call from one of my degree-course students at college, James

Hearsum, asking about the possibility of my putting together a series of lectures on plants. A number of the students were becoming frustrated by how little plantsmanship they were getting as part of their course, and had decided to try to find external expert designers and plantsmen to lecture to them in the evening on specialist topics.

When James spoke to me I was thrilled to think that the students were taking the initiative and doing something about this situation for themselves. I was delighted to be able to help by suggesting various speakers, and by agreeing to give one of the lectures myself, about my world travels. James also managed to attract Chris Beardshaw, Noel Kingsbury, Julie Toll, Peter Seabrook and Ian LeGros. The lectures are spaced a month apart over the winter, which is a great way to give people something to look forward to during the dark evenings.

I'm constantly alarmed by just how long it takes to put together a new lecture. If you think you are going to speak for an hour or an hour and a half, you need to be very focused on what you wish to say and get across. I normally start by just jotting down notes about the subject and only afterwards try to put them into some kind of order. I then look at my vast slide collection to see if I can illustrate what I wish to put over.

I find that for a lecture of this length you need between 60 and 80 slides. Looking through data bases and then looking at the slides is very time-consuming. I also find that, once I am looking at my slides, I may quickly locate the one I want to look at, but I then end up looking at many related ones as they trigger all sorts of memories and I want to immerse myself in the whole experience again. I love doing this in the winter when I have much more time.

Sometimes if I have a free evening I will grab a box of slides, get my equipment set up in my office and transport myself off to some of the magical places that I have been fortunate to travel to over the years. It's a great way of reminding yourself of the lovely plants, people and scenery that you have seen.

*

4 December

I drove up to Newcastle to speak to the north-west group of the Hardy Plant Society in the evening, on 'How to grow 2,000 plants in a 20 x 30 foot garden'. It's my most popular lecture and covers all those planting opportunities that people may not have recognized.

I was greeted at the hall with such friendliness and warmth, with people saying that they felt that they knew me and that we were old friends. This was lovely. A couple had travelled all the way down from Glasgow to hear me and were driving back home at the end of the lecture. I felt very flattered that people would go to so much effort to come and hear me speak.

The lecture was a great success, with lots of laughter coming from my audience, which was nice. As it was the last evening meeting before Christmas, the group served mulled wine and mince pies which were delicious. The couple who were looking after me overnight took me back to their home, and we had a nice meal and a long chat before going to bed. I must admit I was tired.

5 December

I had a good drive home today, but it's a long journey and it took me six hours. When I got in I took Tara for a walk just to relax before getting all my things ready to go over to college, where I was lecturing to my first-year students about soils.

It was strange, because everyone present on this evening was commenting on how tired they felt. On this occasion I had to include myself, and I did find it hard work keeping them motivated and excited. I can tell when I am very tired, as I find it difficult to keep up the enthusiasm for three hours. The students are a nice bunch and all work well together, so I did not have to struggle to get them working in group exercises.

*

6 December

I spent the day at the offices of the Horticultural Trades Association (HTA) in Theale, attending a meeting for those who assess their awards. These are regular meetings in which we look at issues that may have occurred during the year, review assessment methods and discuss the development of good practice. It also allows all the assessors to get together for a chat at least once a year, which is useful.

I got home just in time to go over to college to start my revision sessions with the students who are completing their course with me shortly. It always surprises my students when I talk about technique and presentation in the exams, as they tend to think that all they need is to be able to answer a question. By the end of the evening they were all very aware that there is more to doing a RHS examination than just turning up and sitting the exam.

*

7–9 December

I returned at last to the garden in Little Cambridge to finish clearing the bed of overgrown shrubs and started the replanting.

What became apparent in chatting to Ann, the owner of the garden, was how easy it can be to make the mistake of just ripping everything out and in doing so to remove all the character and established features of a border. When I first discussed the clearing of this border it was suggested that I should remove almost all of what was there. I explained that it might be worth leaving some of the old shrubs in temporarily, and pruning them to shape and removing all the dead, diseased and damaged wood. In this way we could get a clear sight of what was left and, if some shrubs were worth keeping, let them stay.

This is what I did, in practice, to a number of the lilacs and viburnums, and leaving them gave the border a feeling of age, and also some height, which would have been lost if I had followed the original plan and ripped everything away.

The border had been predominantly green, with very little in the way of all-year-round interest, so my new plan was to include plants to increase the season of interest for as long as possible. I went for scented, coloured foliage and winter-flowering plants, plus some evergreens and plants that would flower in the summer.

294

The plants I put in included *Viburnum carlcephalum, Eleagnus* 'Quick Silver' and 'Gilt Edge', *Euonymus alatus, Cotinus* 'Flame', *Physocarpus* 'Diablo', *Nandina domestica, Photinia* 'Red Robin', *Sarcoccoca confusa, Abelia grandiflora, Lonicera fragrantissima,* plus lots of hellebores and grasses. When I had finished the job, Ann seemed delighted and could not believe how much colour was to be enjoyed even at this time of the year. Her reaction pleased me no end, as I know how much more the border will give her over the coming year. It's so nice when you have finished a job and you can see people already enjoying what you have done.

*

10 December

I thought I had better clean out my gutters, as I had not done this in ages and it had been raining very hard. As I've said, I am not keen on being on the top of a 10-m (33-foot) ladder on my own, with no one at the bottom, so I asked my friend Penny to come over to help. We often help each other with jobs like this. Penny will come over here, and I will go over to help her. Some jobs are much easier with two and, in the case of ladder work, so much safer.

I then did some general tidying up of the garden, swept up the leaves which had fallen and removed them from where they were covering plants. This helps prevent rotting, which can occur when decaying leaves lie for a time in the centre of plants. We then took Tara and Indie, Penny's puppy, for a walk.

11 December

Today I had my last class of this term with the Monday group. I was setting them an exam, and they asked if they could sit it in the morning so they could get it out of the way! I did not have a problem with this as the other session of the day, to complete soil texture analysis, could be done at any time.

It was nice to see the students settle down to the exam quickly and to start writing. This is always a good sign. After they had completed the three hours, most said that they felt very relieved that they could answer the questions, and that they had learned a lot since they started the course.

In the afternoon we carried out a hand texture analysis of their own garden soil. This is a good practical as I make them first identify what clay, silt and different types of sandy soils feel like before they test their own soils. The soils are not what they always thought and, as a result, they have been treating them wrongly for years. I explain to them this is why they have not seen the desired results from treatments performed—the soil was wrongly identified in the first place.

This is also a practical class that brings soils alive to the students, and they begin to appreciate that there is a lot to understand about this topic.

During the afternoon break I left the room and, on my return, I found a present from the students on my desk. This rather touched me. I often get presents at the end of a course, but this was the first time in 20 years of teaching that I was given a Christmas present. It was a bottle of my favourite malt whisky, along with a lovely home-made card taking the mickey out of an article that I had written, about rats hiding under decking, which had produced a lot of interest. It is so nice when you get a class of students who have a great sense of humour.

*

12 December

I spent a lot of the day writing and preparing for the lecture 'Plants from around the world' which James Hearsum had asked me to give. The lecture attracted about 240 people, and they seemed to enjoy seeing slides of my travels and hearing how to grow some of these fascinating plants.

What was interesting about the evening was that many of my past students turned up, so it was a bit like a reunion. Several other people commented that they had seen *Christine's Garden* and were quite amazed to discover that I had such a great depth of knowledge. I was wasted on this type of TV, they said! I explained to them that the series was about my passion and enthusiasm rather than showing off my knowledge.

*

13 December

Louise took me down to the railway station and I caught the train into London. At Liverpool Street station I was met by a car which took me to the television studios at White City, where I was to take part in Channel 4's *Paul O'Grady Show*. This was the first time that Paul had discussed gardening on the show, and it turned out to be fun.

When I first arrived, I was shown into a dressing-room and was told that we would do a rehearsal,

297

just to check positions and so on. This was done without any plants, etc., and took the form of me chatting to the floor manager rather than to Paul. After I had done this I was shown back to my dressing-room.

After a while there was a knock on the door. It was Paul, who had come to introduce himself and have a chat. He was so nice. He complimented me on my 'wonderful' series and was obviously very taken with it. We chatted about his animals and how he produces his own food, milk and cream. We were soon talking like old friends.

The seven-minute slot was very funny, with me just chatting naturally and asking Paul to do the actual work. We had a good laugh together, and it turned out to be great fun. I also got Robert Powell and Sarah Alexander, Paul's other guests on the show, doing a bit of pruning as well.

I got home and went round to Reg and Louise to tell them that the programme would be shown tomorrow, not tonight. This was a pity as Louise had already opened some wine and had some lovely nibbles ready. Alas, we drank the wine and ate the nibbles and said we would just have to watch it without them tomorrow night!

*

14 December
Busy in the office all day doing admin and writing. Then I went round to Louise's to watch the *Paul O'Grady Show*, but did not have anything to drink as I was going off to college immediately after the show. We all laughed at what was shown, including a clip from the first series of Reg, Louise and myself chatting about watering. I was pleased with

how it all came across.

I got back into the house and, in the half-hour between the end of the show and my leaving to go to college, several people phoned to say how good it was and that I should feel very proud of myself. Rupert phoned and was great. He said it was brilliant, and that it was obvious that Paul and I had a good rapport, and that I should perhaps do more with Paul because it came across very well.

Over to college for the evening, and my final session with this group of students. We continued looking at exam revision and technique. After the class we went to a local pub and said our farewells.

*

15 December

I went over to prune Brigid's roses at Buckhurst Hill. It was a cold, bright day and, while I was working out at the front of the flats, several people stopped when they recognized me and commented that they did not expect to see me actually gardening now that I had been on television. I replied that I had a living to make and television only occupies part of the year.

Tara had to go to the vet's for her annual MOT in the evening. I hate this, as I always wonder and worry that they will find something wrong with her. She had an examination and the vet said she was fine. He gave her the annual booster and off we went. I must say I felt rather relieved. Tara always gets a bowl of her favourite biscuits when she gets back, as a treat. I love to see her tucking into these. It makes me feel less guilty about having to put her through it. She is not the only one who does not like these visits!

16–17 December

I had a sociable weekend, visiting friends and showing them slides of trips that I had been on, and getting them up to date on the filming and how I have spent this year. They all commented that I should not really be surprised to feel tired with everything that has happened.

I took Tara for a long walk along the river and noticed that the oak trees have now, finally, lost all their leaves. The landscape looks bare, and now the true shapes of trees and shrubs are completely revealed. I love days when it is cold and crisp and the trees stand out against the fields. I think of them as guardian angels keeping an eye on everything around, and looking after the countryside. People often think that winter is a dull time of the year. They should go out and look really closely at what is there in nature. It should make them think again.

*

18 December

I returned to Brigid's to finish all the pruning and general tidying up of the gardens. It was a bitterly cold damp day and I just got colder and colder. I have not got my thermals out yet, as it had been so mild, but today really caught me out. I must say, I was so cold that I did not really enjoy the day and was very glad to get home and into the warm. It is surprising how much better a good soak in a hot bath can make you feel.

After dinner I took Tara over to Penny's, where I've decided to stay the night. It will be easier for me to get to my appointment in Theale tomorrow from there than it would from home, as I would have had to leave so early because of the motorway traffic.

∗

19 December
Another meeting at the HTA offices in Theale. We discussed some training the organization is offering to support the HTA awards for the horticultural industry. The aim of the meeting was to bring all the trainers together so that we could discuss how we were going to deliver these training sessions to ensure standardization across the regions, and to consider the course content.

This was a very useful meeting and we achieved a great deal. I think these new courses will really help candidates with their preparation for the exam and the practical assessment. I came away from the meeting feeling that it had been thoroughly worthwhile.

∗

20 December
We had the first serious frost last night, and anything that had been surviving so far has now turned to mush. I spent most of the day in the garden removing the frosted foliage and generally cleaning up. All of this material was placed into black bags and will go into the compost bins once I have had the opportunity to empty them.

The birds were busy feeding, and it was lovely to see so many tits and robins feeding happily while I was working only a few feet away. There is something very satisfying about a freezing cold day

301

and being out in a garden, keeping moving to stay warm.

In the afternoon I made myself a hot toddy, sat on my bench and looked at the garden, thinking how strange that this is where two series of *Christine's Garden* have been made. In many ways it still does not feel real or possible, yet because I am so tired after all of this year's activities, it makes me realize just how demanding filming is.

I spent the evening writing.

*

21 December

Sue Dougan, from BBC Kent, turned up to record an interview that will be inserted into a live three-hour show I am doing with her on Christmas Eve. We chatted about the past year, all the things that have occurred and the highs and lows of filming. It is a nice piece, which hopefully will give a flavour of what this demanding year has been like.

In the afternoon I went Christmas shopping. This was my first opportunity to get myself organized. Fortunately for me, the shops were on the empty side. This was good, as I hate shopping and only go when I absolutely have to. It is usually the fact that I have to get Tara some food that takes me out shopping. I grow all my own vegetables, make my own bread and have grown very inventive at making things from ingredients in my store cupboard.

The evening was spent wrapping presents and getting into the spirit of the season. Carols were playing; I had opened a bottle of wine and was joining in. Funnily enough, I can never remember the words. I think this is because I learned to play the recorder, and therefore know the music better than the words. I still play the recorder, and sometimes join a group of children carol-singing. I just love playing with them and seeing their faces as people open their doors to see and hear us. Music is such a great way of getting all the ages together in an enjoyable manner.

*

22 December

I spent some time in the garden painting the fences. This is not a job I like but, when you are on your own, you have to turn your hand to anything and everything. I hate seeing fences in disrepair and looking tatty. It does take time, as many of my panels have plants growing on them, which have to be taken down to allow me to paint the fence. I normally just support the plants by placing bricks underneath them. I will put the plants back up in the morning when the paint is dry.

In the afternoon I popped round to see a client just up the road to do half a day's rose pruning for her. She only has 50 bushes, so it was not a big job, but she is now getting to the age where she's not able to do them herself. It's lovely seeing clients at this time of the year, as you get fed mince pies and tea during the day. What is that story of having to have a mince pie in 12 different houses before Christmas? Well I can tell you that I can beat that several times over by now!

In the evening I watched another repeated episode of *Christine's Garden* shown on BBC2. I am now able to watch this without feeling very odd, and I enjoyed what I saw this evening.

*

23 December

I reattached all the plants to the fence and tied in any outward-facing growth before travelling to BBC Essex to do my regular two-hour spot with Ken Crowther.

We generally just chatted about the fact that, being a traditionalist, I do not like the commercial aspect of Christmas but I do like the real side.

I decorate my house with living plant material and I have a real Christmas tree. I just love stockings filled with nuts, fruit, chocolate, miniatures of different single malt whiskies and different small cheeses. I often have to do this myself, as I'm on my own and Santa does not come down my chimney, and not many people know that this is something that I enjoy very much. (They will now—look out next Christmas, Christine!)

*

24 December

I left the house at 6.30 a.m. to drive down to BBC Kent in Tunbridge Wells. I did a three-hour live radio phone-in with Sue Dougan, which was most enjoyable. Lots of questions about how to look after plants given as Christmas presents, what pruning should be done at this time of the year, what new varieties had taken my fancy and which I would I grow this coming season. Also, what had it been like filming a second series, and what did I want out of 2007? I enjoyed being with Sue very much, and I appreciated the regular callers, who listen to me on BBC Essex, phoning in just to say they could pick up BBC Kent.

Returned home and walked Tara, and then

made my way over to see my friend Marie, who is a great cook. She only saw me recently, but on that occasion we were joined by a friend who does not enjoy fish, so Maria said to come back today and she would cook me some fish, and I could also see her slides of Egypt.

Marie, who is from Spain, is the most wonderful cook and always does me proud. She loves fish herself, so it is a double pleasure joining her in something she really enjoys as well.

I have known Marie since we completed our Certificates in Education together many years ago. She is interested in art and used to lecture on the subject, and, like me, she travels widely. Marie travels the world to look at rock art, churches and buildings. She has the most fascinating collection of slides, which I enjoy seeing.

*

25 December

As it is Christmas Day I treated myself to a breakfast of scrambled eggs and smoked salmon washed down with champagne. I look forward to this breakfast during the run-up to Christmas. I took Tara for a walk down by the river, and then joined Louise and Colin on a visit to friends for nibbles and champagne. Louise had invited me, plus six others, for Christmas dinner, and we had a lovely day. We opened presents from each other, chatted about the year and generally just relaxed over a lovely traditional Christmas dinner.

This is what Christmas is to me. Friends together, having a simple but great time, eating nice food, drinking lovely wines and just enjoying each other's company. What could be better?

*

26–31 December

Most of the time was spent visiting friends and walking Tara. I love seeing friends and just being part of their families.

I spent some time reflecting on a marvellous year. When total strangers approached me with such warmth, it reaffirmed my belief in humanity. I even coped with being recognized much better than I had anticipated.

Christine's Garden obviously meant a lot to many people. It was a great success and I had spent the entire year being told about it. In practice there have only been three days out of the whole year when someone has not approached me and made a lovely comment about the series, and about Reg, Louise and Tara.

I leave 2006 with so many mixed memories. I doubt very much if I will ever experience this type of roller coaster journey again.

On reflection it has been worth the effort. I was so unsure when making the first series. This year, however, the doubts and worries I had just seemed to melt away. It was the kind comments from the public that really made me appreciate what it has meant to so many. I know what my garden, and life, means to me. What has been marvellous is having the opportunity to share this with so many others.

The second series has, in some ways, been easier to make and, in others, equally difficult. I do not think I will ever get used to having people in my home and garden. But being able to work with true professionals at the BBC has been a great honour and pleasure. They have brought a new understanding of television to me. I now see it with very different eyes.

The opportunity of sharing my year with the readers of this book has also been a pleasure. Time will tell if you enjoy it as much as the television series. I hope so, as the greatest gift a person can have is being able to share a passion and enthusiasm for their subject with others. Whatever else you do, keep gardening and enjoying Mother Nature. She is the most marvellous thing on the planet Earth.

CHIVERS
LARGE
PRINT
−direct−

If you have enjoyed this Large Print book and would like to build up your own collection of Large Print books, please contact

Chivers Large Print Direct

Chivers Large Print Direct offers you a full service:

● Prompt mail order service

● Easy-to-read type

● The very best authors

● Special low prices

For further details either call Customer Services on (01225) 336552 or write to us at Chivers Large Print Direct, **FREEPOST**, Bath BA1 3ZZ

Telephone Orders: **FREEPHONE** 08081 72 74 75